A Simpler Guide to Gmail

Getting the most out of Google's free email

Ceri Clark

A Simpler Guide to Gmail: Getting the most out of Google's free email

Published by
Lycan Books
1 Monet Crescent, Newport, NP19 7PP
www.lycanbooks.com

ISBN: 1-909236-00-4
ISBN-13: 978-1-909236-00-4

DEDICATION

To all my family and friends who needed help and advice on using Google's Gmail which persuaded me to write this book.

CONTENTS

ACKNOWLEDGMENTS

I would like to thank Google for creating such wonderful online software and for allowing it to be used for free.

Chapter 1 Introduction

There are a myriad of email solutions on the internet, some of them are free, others charge and a few are a combination of the two. This is a no-nonsense step-by-step guide which aims to show you how to get the most out of Google's solution, Gmail.

Why Gmail?

In my opinion, Google offers the best service for email. My reasons are:

- Easy to use

- Over 7 gigabytes of space (enough for a lifetime of email)

- Spell Checking

- Address Book (Contacts)

- Mobile access (for your iPhone or Android mobile phone, although any phone capable of using a browser can use it)

- Possibly *the* best spam (unwanted email) protection in the world!

Ceri Clark

For the purposes of this guide, I have made a few assumptions. The first is that you have (or at least have access to) a computer, you are familiar with using a mouse and know what the internet is.

Setting up your Google Gmail Account

First the easy bit. Head over to the Account set up page. As in (a) in Figure 1 below, type in your address bar: http://mail.google.com/.

Figure 1.1 Creating an account

Google will redirect you to the right place. Please click on **Create an account** (b) as shown in Figure 1 above.

You will then be taken to the page as illustrated in Figure 1.2 below to open a Google Account:

Figure 1.2 Sign-in form

Opening a Google account doesn't just give you email, by creating this account you can use all Google services with one username and password...

Filling in the Form

Make sure you fill in all the boxes that are required.

Choosing your Username

Your username is your new email address. I recommend choosing something that you won't be embarrassed about later. You may apply for jobs or be using this email address in your business. Fluffywuffychocolateguzzler may sound funny and may even be free when you type it in but future employers or business contacts may not be so impressed!

The idea is to create an address of the form <username>@gmail.com where you are picking the <username> bit before the @ symbol.

When you put in your desired username, Google will automatically check to see if it is available, if not the following will appear:

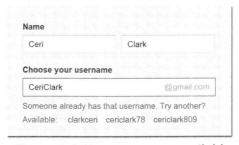

Figure 1.3 Username not available

Notice the nice people at Google have given you a few pointers below your choices for some names that *are* available? You can choose one of those but being a bit more creative can look more appropriate than putting a number on the end. For example if you have put in your abbreviated first name, then your full first name may be more suitable or even putting in your middle name.

Type in different variants or choose one of their suggestions until one becomes available.

Choosing your Password

Next choose a password, making sure that it is strong. There are a few schools of thought when it comes to passwords. Here I am going to cover four ways.

No. 1 The simplest one to remember is choosing three random words which mean something to you but would be impossible to guess for an outsider. For example, if your favorite food is cake, your favorite holiday was in Hawaii and you just love baseball, then as much as my spell check hates it, cakeHawaiibaseball could be considered an excellent password.

No. 2 Another way to choose a password is by using a combination of letters, numbers and special characters. Using everyday words can make it easy to remember. For example, **Elephantsrock** is bad, **El3ph@nt5r0ck** is strong. To get El3ph@nt5r0ck, (as if you haven't already worked it out!), I replaced an e with 3, the a with @, s with 5 and o with 0 (zero). All the replacement numbers look like their letter counterparts to make it easy to remember.

No. 3 The third way is to choose a phrase which you will remember and take the first letters of each word. For example, *The scariest movie I have seen is Omen*! Once you have settled on a phrase just add a special character and number, I saw the film when I was about 9 so that's the number I will choose here. This password would be Tsmihsi0!9.

No. 4 The final way to choose a password is similar to the above method but involves an aid. Those familiar with the movie, *Unknown* with Liam Neeson may recognize this. If you have a favorite book then choose a passage and from that passage choose a word. For example, if the word is in the 22nd line on page 150. 2

words along and the word is mammoth, the word would be 150222mammoth, or any combination of these elements.

A good way to cheat is to use a service such as LastPass. Sign up at lastpass.com and use their service to generate passwords for you. You will need one password to use LastPass but the service will remember all your other passwords and this way you can have different passwords for all the websites you visit and only have to remember the one!

Birthday, Gender and Mobile Phone

The first two are self-explanatory, although if you are hyper-sensitive about your birthday I have known people to put a different birthday in. If you do this, remember what you entered!

Your mobile phone will be used to text a code to prove who you are if you need to reset your account if you have forgotten your password.

Word Verification (prove you are not a robot)

Otherwise known as CAPTCHA this is required to stop computers automatically creating accounts and using them to spam people. Type in the word you see or click on the wheelchair icon to hear an audio version.

Location

Choose the country where you currently reside. This will make sure that your emails have the correct date and time for where you are. If the wrong location is set it could look like you are time travelling in the past to send emails. Another reason to choose the right location is to make sure you have the right terms and conditions for your country.

Terms of Service

Make sure you read the Terms of Service and then click on **Next step.**

Create your Profile

For the next step you need to create your profile. This will not only improve your Gmail experience but it will be your passport to other Google services.

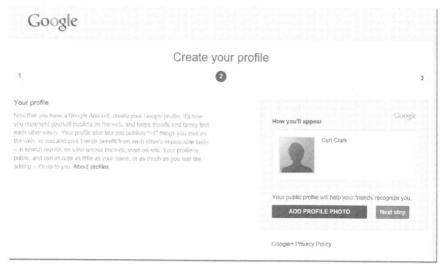

Figure 1.4 Create your profile

Adding your profile picture

First add your profile picture by clicking the **Add Profile Picture** button as in Figure 1.4 above.

Your profile picture can be anything you want within reason. Obviously celebrity photos or indecent images would not be suitable but if you want to use the picture of a goldfish – go for it!

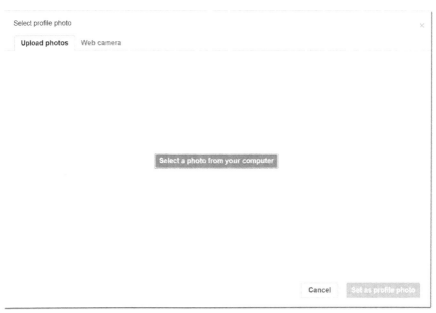

Figure 1.5 Create your profile

You have a choice of either picking a photo from your computer or taking a photo with your webcam. You can flip from one option to the other by clicking on the tabs as can be seen in the above figure.

To select a picture from your computer, choose the aptly named button at the center of the screen and then navigate to where you store your photos, usually **My Pictures** in Windows. Click on the photo you want and then choose **Open**.

The browser window will be replaced by another showing your profile picture as in figure 1.6 below. You can crop the image (choose only a part of the whole image) by 'grabbing' one of the little white squares on each corner of the smoky glass effect square on top. To do this, left-click on the little square and pull the mouse towards you to make the square bigger and away to make it smaller.

You can move the selecting square by placing your mouse pointer over the square and left clicking. Keep your finger on the left mouse button and drag to where you want it.

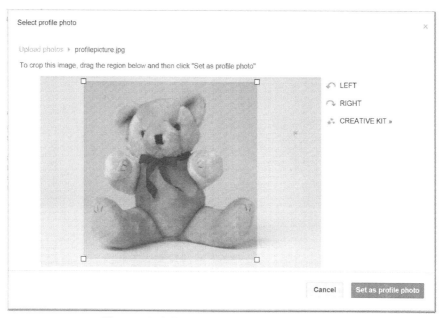

Figure 1.6 Cropping your profile picture

By clicking on **left** and **right** (to the side of your profile picture), the image will rotate. Advanced options can be found by clicking **Creative Kit**.

You can also crop in the Creative Kit section as well as add special effects, such as making your photograph look like an old Polaroid. A nice touch is the ability to put writing on your photo but this is really just a gimmick. Once you have completed all the options choose **Set as profile photo**.

If you choose to take a picture with your camera, then click on the web camera tab (see Figure 1.6 above). You may get a message stating that plus.google.com is asking for your camera and microphone access. This is fine, click the **Allow** button. Once the new page has loaded, you just have to click on take a snapshot, once or twice, maybe three times if you are like me. Choose the photo you are most happy with and then click on **Set as profile photo**. If you already have a photo that you would like to upload already on the computer click **cancel**.

Once you chosen your profile picture, click on **Next step**.

Congratulations you now have a Google email address!

Figure 1.7 You have now set up your account

Click on **Continue to Gmail...**

Chapter 2 Getting Started

The first thing you might see is a Google video talking about new features that Google has implemented. I recommend you have a look at this.

If there is no video or when you close it, the screen you see will look like Figure 2.1 below. First of all don't panic. It isn't as complicated as it looks!

Figure 2.1 Email home screenshot

11

As you can see there are four emails even before you've told all your best mates about your new address. These hold links to customizing the look and feel, importing your contacts and old email from other email services and using your mobile to see your email.

Logging in

Some time has flown by and you haven't checked your email. You click open your browser, probably Internet Explorer, Chrome or Firefox. The horror, it's logged you out, how do I check it now?

Going directly there

Depending on if you bought this as a paperback or ebook, you could type in the following website address or highlight and copy it

http://mail.google.com

...and paste it into the address bar. Press Enter on your keyboard (otherwise known as Return) and you will be taken directly there.

Figure 2.2 Address bar

Fill in the boxes as in Figure 2.3, click on **Sign in** and you will be in to your email. Remember, the username box needs to be your whole email address. In the example cases in this book it would be cericlarkexample@gmail.com.

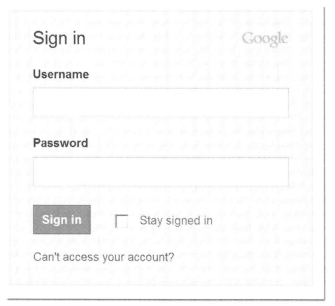

Figure 2.3 Login box

Check the box next to **Stay signed in** to avoid typing in your password every day. Remember do NOT do this if you use a shared computer as other people would then have access to your account.

Adding Google as your homepage

If the first thing you do each day is check your Gmail account I recommend putting iGoogle as your homepage. If you are using Internet Explorer click on the little gear wheel on the top right of your window, Choose **Internet Options** and then type http://www.google.co.uk/ig if you are in the UK and http://www.google.com/ig if you are in the US (adjust as necessary for other countries). Once you have done this click on **OK** and iGoogle will be the first page you see when you load your browser. Selecting the little house icon on the top right of your browser will also bring up iGoogle from now on.

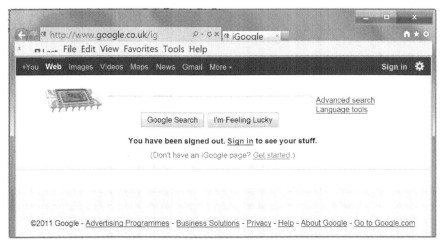

Figure 2.4 iGoogle not signed in

To get to your Gmail account, find **Gmail** in the black bar (although it is seventh in figure 2.4, the location does change within the bar) and click on it. The page as shown in Figure 2.3 will load. Type in your username and password and choose **Sign in**.

Reading Emails

This is the reason you created the account, right? Well this couldn't be simpler. As with every other email service out there, you just click anywhere on the email. The emails are displayed with who sent it first, the subject (what the email is about) and then the date it arrives. I'm interested in customizing with colors and themes so I click on the **Customize Gmail with colors and themes** subject.

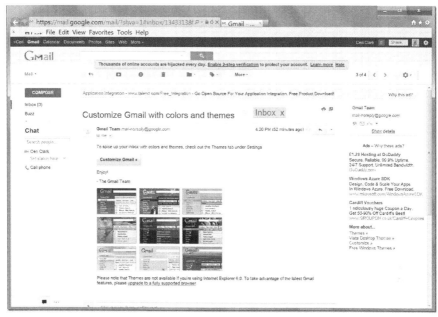

Figure 2.5 An example email

Images are sometimes blocked by Google. This is done to protect your computer but you can change this by changing the settings. If you would like to see the images in a particular email and it is blocked, Google will let you know as shown in Figure 2.6.

Figure 2.6 Displaying images in emails

Click on **Display images below** to see the email as it was meant to be viewed.

Once you have read the email, you can click on inbox (or the Gmail logo) to send you right back to the home screen.

Notice that once you have read an email, it greys out.

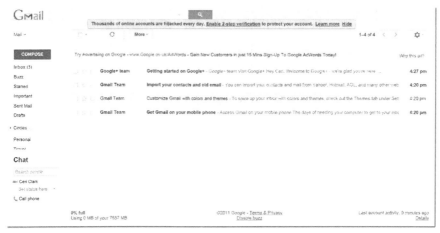

Figure 2.7 A read email grays out

To delete the email, click on the small box to the left of the email and then click on the picture of a trashcan above it. If you hover your mouse over the pictures, a little message pops up telling you what the picture means. I will go into more detail in the next chapter.

Figure 2.8 Trashcan image for deleting emails

Viewing Attachments

With Gmail you can look at attachments from right inside your browser. This means that if you don't have the software on your computer then you can still see most documents.

How do they do this? You will have to activate the Google Docs service as it opens the attachment in Google Docs. This means that you can view most documents as long as you have a) access to the internet and b) access to a browser.

Figure 2.9 shows how Google displays what documents are attached to the email and the options available. As you can see, you can download them individually or all three at the same time.

You get a preview of images but by clicking on **View** a full size image will load. Clicking on **View** next to documents will allow you to see them in in Google Documents. If you don't happen to have Microsoft Word but you still want to see what a document says, then this could be your answer. If Google Docs does not support the attachment file type, in the below example a Mobi file, you can download the file on to your computer and use software from there. In this case Kindle for PC or Calibre.

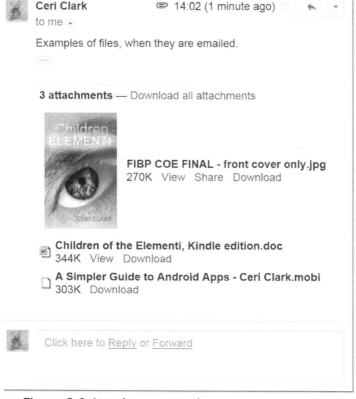

Figure 2.9 Attachments as they appear in an email

Turn off Chat

If you are new to Google then there is plenty of time to find out more but to reduce the risk of information overload I recommend you turn off Chat

You can always reactivate it later, but for now there's so much to concentrate on.

First, go to the gear wheel at the top right of the screen, this is the settings button, as in figure 2.10.

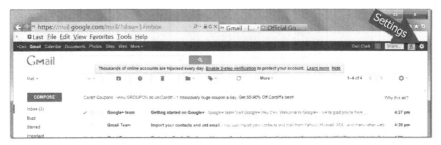

Figure 2.10 Location of settings button

A dropdown menu will appear when it is clicked on allowing you to choose **Mail settings** to get the following screen.

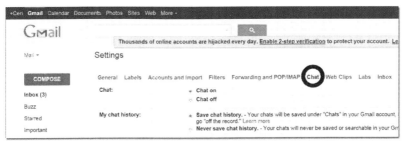

Figure 2.11 Chat settings

Go to the circled location labeled chat (as above) to get all the settings relevant to Chat. Turn chat off by choosing **Chat off** and then clicking **Save Changes** at the bottom of the screen.

Reactivating Chat

If you would like to do this later, follow the steps in turning it off but choose **Chat on**.

Ceri Clark

Chapter 3 Security

Securing your Google account is very important. Identity theft is a growing problem on the internet and you need to protect yourself as much as possible.

Your Browser Connection

Make sure that **Always use https** is selected in the **General Settings**.

To get to General Settings as always go to the gear wheel on the top right of the Google screen and then choose settings. Search for Browser Connection at the bottom of the list.

If you hold down the Ctrl and F keys at the same time, a find box will load on your Windows computer (or CMD and F on a Mac). Type what you want to search for, example Browser Connection and you will be taken to the text in the page instantly. This saves you scrolling for what you are looking for.

Passwords

I go into detail about this in Chapter One in the section called Choosing your password. Please read this for ways of choosing your password.

Changing your password

To change your password at any time, go to the settings page, then **Accounts and Import**. The **Change Password** link is the first item in the page.

Two-factor authentication

Changing your password regularly is a good way of securing access to your account, but remembering hundreds of passwords, constantly changing, can be a headache. Google's two-step verification can be an elegant solution to this.

2-step verification/authentication is an extra step to make sure that access to your information, files and folders is restricted to you. Instead of relying just on a password, a secondary device is used which you always have on you such as a phone or tablet computer. Any would-be infiltrator, bent on your destruction would need to have your password AND your phone to gain access to your account.

How to setup 2-step verification on Google

I recommend you follow the instructions below for setting up the 2-step verification in the order as set out below because of the complicated nature of setting it up.

Go to **Settings** again > **Accounts and Import** > **Other Google Account Settings**.

The following page will load:

Figure 3.1 Location of 2-step verification

Click on **Edit** on the 2-step verification line and you will be directed to login in again. Once you do you will be taken to the page to setup the verification.

Type in your mobile/cell number in the space provided as illustrated in the next figure, choose how you want the code to be sent to you. I chose SMS text verification. Click **Send verification** and the code will be texted to you. Take the code from your phone and enter it in the space provided in the form and click **Verify**.

Figure 3.2 Setting up 2-steo verification

Google will then give you a verification screen asking you if you want to be remembered on this computer for 30 days. Only choose this if you do **not** share your computer with others.

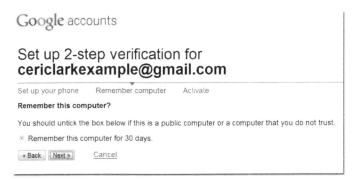

Figure 3.3 2-step verification screen. Choose this only if you or people you trust has access to your computer.

When you click **Next** another verification screen will appear:

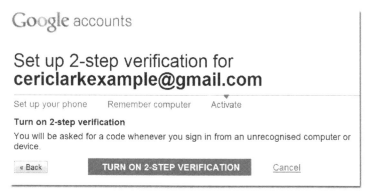

Figure 3.4 Final verification screen for 2-step verification

Click on **TURN ON 2-STEP AUTHENTICATION**. You will be directed to login again.

If you use apps on mobile devices for any Google service, you will need to have application specific passwords to be able to access Google from them. *If you only access Google from your computer you do not have to worry about application specific passwords.*

Google will recognize your use of a mobile device and warn you that you will need to generate some passwords, that will only need to be inputted once for each application on a device. Click on **Create passwords** on the bottom of the screen that has loaded.

Figure 3.5 One time passwords will need to be generated for apps

You will of course be asked to login again.

I use my Gmail account on my Smartphone and Tablet for the MailDroid email application. To generate a password for this, I typed **MailDroid** in the box provided in the page that loaded.

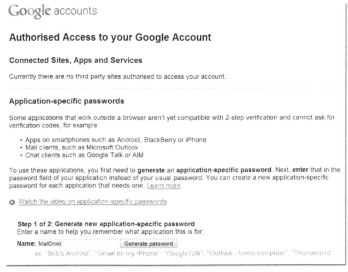

Figure 3.6 Generating passwords for apps

Once you have typed the application name click on **Generate password**. On the next screen your one time only password will appear as illustrated in the next figure:

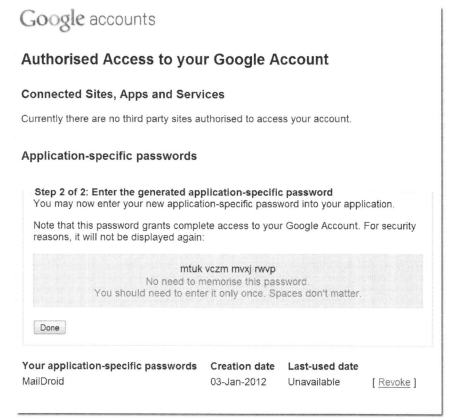

Figure 3.7 2-step authentication passwords generated screen

Notice that the application that you specified appears at the bottom of the screen? This is the beginning of a list of passwords you will have to generate for every application on all your mobile devices that you want to connect to Google. Google allows you to Revoke the password at any time by logging into your account. By doing this, if you lose your phone/tablet or other device then you can delete the passwords stopping anyone from accessing your account from that device.

If you have more than one device where you use the same application (for example, MailDroid on a tablet *and* a phone) I would recommend you that you put the device name in the application name you chose. For example, I used MailDroid but if you have it on more than one device you could use MailDroidPhone or MailDroidTablet depending on your preference.

Now that you have your password, type it in to the password field of the application that you want to use.

For MailDroid, I clicked on the email address, chose **Edit** and typed in the confirmation code without spaces into the password field. I was able to refresh the email as normal.

A word of warning, if you use MailDroid or another application that downloads your email, even if you use 2-step verification, someone can access information already downloaded. Even if there is no generated password in the application then information already on there can still be accessed but they won't be able to download new emails, therefore 2-step authentication should not be used as a replacement for password protecting your device.

Accessing 2-step authentication after setup

To go back into your 2-step authentication go to:

Settings > Accounts and Import > Other Google Account Settings.

Click on **Edit**, next to 2-step verification and you will be taken to the master control page.

Figure 3.8 2-step verification administration page

The most important information on this page are the backup verification codes. You need to use these if you have 2-step verification enabled but you don't have access to your phone for any reason.

To generate more application specific passwords, simply click on **Manage application specific passwords**.

Using an Android app to gain verification codes

Every 30 days you will be asked to relogin, this also happens if you use a computer you haven't used before. You can get codes by SMS or using an Android app. This section explains how to use **Google Authenticator**.

Figure 3.9 Google Authenticator on the Marketplace

First install "Google Authenticator" from Google Play (formerly the Android Market) on your Android device, or App Store on your iPhone.

Next go back to your 2-step verification administration panel by going to Settings > Accounts and Import > Other Google Account Settings.

Click on **Edit**, next to 2-step verification and you will be taken to the master control page.

Next to **Mobile Application**, choose **Android**. If you are using an iPhone or Blackberry, follow the on-screen instructions for those devices.

A page will load with a barcode.

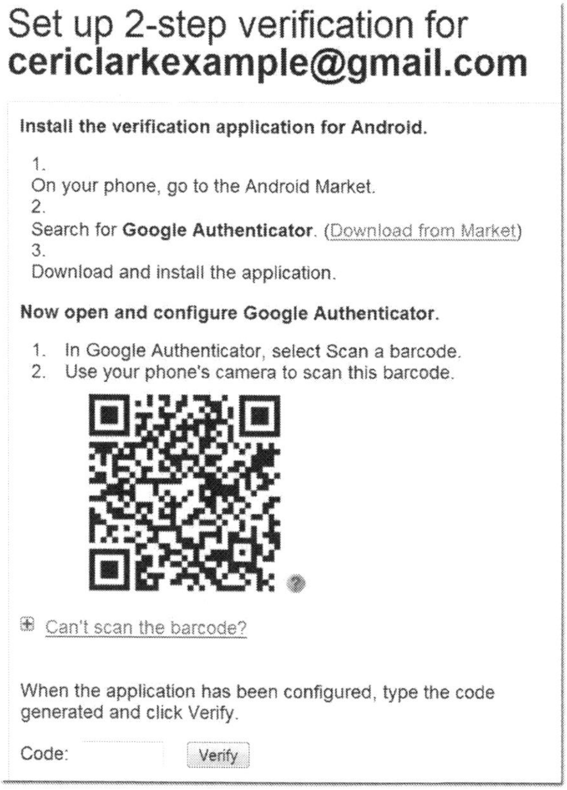

Set up 2-step verification for cericlarkexample@gmail.com

Install the verification application for Android.

1.
On your phone, go to the Android Market.
2.
Search for **Google Authenticator**. (Download from Market)
3.
Download and install the application.

Now open and configure Google Authenticator.

1. In Google Authenticator, select Scan a barcode.
2. Use your phone's camera to scan this barcode.

⊕ Can't scan the barcode?

When the application has been configured, type the code generated and click Verify.

Code: [   ]   [Verify]

Figure 3.10 Mobile app authentication page

Go back to your mobile device and choose **Scan a barcode**.

Goggles or another barcode scanning application will load. If you don't have a barcode reader already on your device, search for barcode reader on Google Play and download.

Use the camera on your device to view the barcode on the computer screen. Google Authenticator will then give you a unique code to type into the **Code** at the bottom of the barcode page of the Google Authentication setup webpage.

Figure 3.11 Google Authenticator code from a mobile device

After you click **Verify** on your computer you will receive a message to say your Android device is configured.

If you find that it doesn't work after a few attempts, check the time and time-zone is correct on your device(s). Embarrassingly I made this mistake the first time I did it.

Chapter 4 Sending and receiving emails

Emails are dealt with a little differently in Gmail from some other email services. As long as the subject is the same, everything in one conversation is held in one place. No more searching through your Sent folder to find what you said! This section talks about how to send email but also how the discussion threads work.

Discussions

Discussion threads are conversations. Please see Figure 4.1 below for an example. If I have sent the email from this Gmail account then it will appear as **me**. Once read, it will go grey as illustrated below.

Figure 4.1 Example of a discussion thread

Notice next to **Ceri**, the number lets me know how many emails are in the discussion. If anyone sends me an email later, it will revert to white (until I click on it) and the two will become a three. Next to the subject Google has also put some of the first line of the email, so I can decide if I want to read it or not.

Click anywhere on the row and it will take you to the conversation.

A thread will look like this:

Figure 4.2 Example of an email thread

If you are not sure which is the latest email, look at the date at the top right of each email, which also tells you how long ago the email was sent.

Replying and forwarding an email

Replying to an email is as simple as clicking on **Reply**! Google has made this extra easy by giving us two places to use this. At the top of the email on the right hand corner there is a grey box with an arrow in it as seen in figure 4.3. Clicking on this will bring up a drop-down list. The top option will be **Reply**. Of course there is always the **Reply** at the foot of each email beside **Forward**.

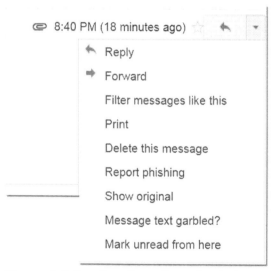

Figure 4.3 Email options from Reply button

The reply box looks as below. Type in the white spaces and then click Send. You could always save what you have written so far by clicking on **Save Now**. You will then be able to find it again in **Drafts** later, at the left of the screen, or the other option is to **Discard** what you have written.

The convention is to write your reply above the message you are replying to. This means that your correspondent does not have to go looking for your answer. If you are replying to a friend then this does not matter as they will love you enough to go looking for your reply, but if you are using your email for business, you do not want to annoy your customers/contacts before they have even read your message.

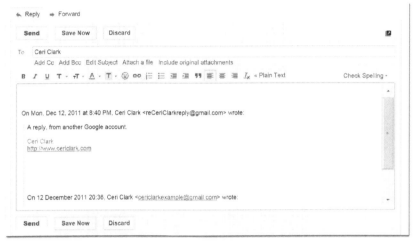

Figure 4.4 Reply screen

You will get a message highlighted in yellow to tell you it has been sent.

Forwarding uses the same method but you will have to put in the email address of the person you want it to go to.

The options for formatting an email will appear in the Composing an email section below.

If you want to reply or forward to a particular message rather than the whole thread, choose the box the message is in from the thread and click the Reply button on that particular message. You can choose not to include quoted text.

Composing an email

Composing an email is a simple process, in the first column of the page, click on the box labeled **Compose**. See below for what it looks like.

Figure 4.5 Where to find Compose (mail)

The Compose Mail page will load, ready for you to fill in.

Ceri Clark

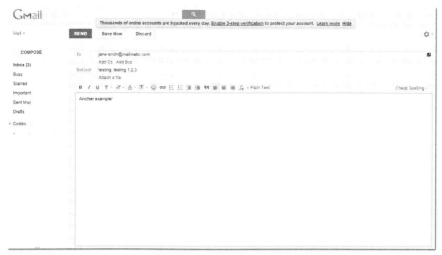

Figure 4.6 Example of the Compose mail box

Clicking on the **To** will bring up your address book but I am assuming you don't have one yet. If you know the email address, just type it into the white box. Then type in a descriptive subject and what you want to say in the large box. If you are ready click **Send**.

Formatting your email

You might think your email is a tad boring without formatting. As in a lot of word processors you can change the way an email looks and feels by highlighted what you want changed and clicking the B for Bold button as I did in the example below or any of the other formatting options. If you are not sure what the buttons do, then move your mouse over them and a brief explanation will appear next to it.

below.

Formatting your emails can make them easier to read. Bold your headings to make sure people take notice of what is important.

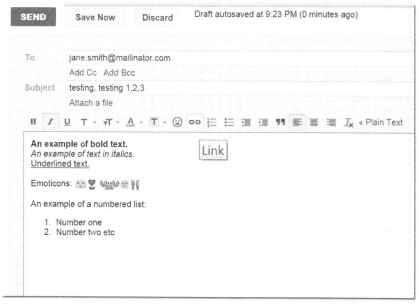

Figure 4.7 The formatting bar after the mouse is hovered over a button

Adding a link to your email

To add a link to the main body of text click on the little picture that looks like a chain above the word link as in figure 4.7 above. Fill in the **Edit Link** box and click on **OK**.

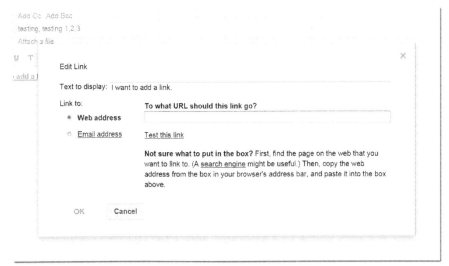

Figure 4.8 Adding a link to your email

Spell Check

Spell Check is an amazing tool which Google provides for free. To take advantage of this feature click on **Check Spelling** (on the same line as the formatting options such as Bold, italicize etc.).

Once clicked, the spelling mistakes will be highlighted in yellow as shown in figure 4.9 below.

Figure 4.9 Spell checking

To see Google's suggestions and correct the spelling mistakes, click on the highlighted text.

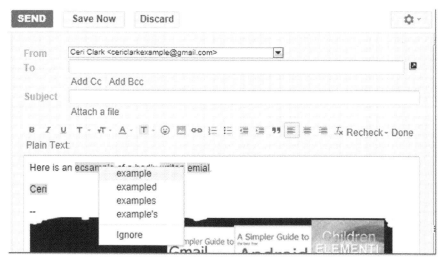

Figure 4.10 Example of a spell check list

Once a misspelt word is clicked, a list of options appears. Select which one you think is right and click on it. The word will be replaced and the yellow highlighting will disappear.

Deleting an email

To delete messages before they are sent click on **Discard**. To delete emails that are sent to you, first go to the homepage of the email by clicking on the Gmail logo, then click on the little box to the left of the email. This adds a tick to the box, and then click on the trashcan icon which will appear above your emails list.

Chapter 5 Address Book (Google Contacts)

Keeping all your contacts online is a great idea. As well as saving on paper, it also means that you can update your contacts wherever you are, whether at home or on a mobile device when travelling. It is all about convenience.

How to add contacts using the Gmail website

First go to the contacts page, this is usually under **Mail** and above **Compose**. Please see Figure 5.1 for a visual clue. Google has a habit of moving things around but in the version at the time of writing the Contacts link can be found by clicking on the little arrow next to **Mail** at the top left of the screen as in figure 5.1.

Figure 5.1 Contacts location on home screen

Once the page has loaded click on **New Contact** on the left of the screen.

The first thing you should do is click on **Add name**, once you do this you just need to start typing the name and click out of the box when you are done.

If you are not happy with what you have written or want to add more detail you can hover your mouse over the name and click on the three dots which appear. Click on those three dots and a window will load as in figure 5.2 with more lovely fields to fill in. If you are of a pedantic disposition, then this is wonderful as you can specify a prefix like Mrs, Ms, Mr etc or even a suffix like PhD. In my example, I've awarded my fictional character an OBE from the

Queen. I have a high class of fictional friends. ☺ Once the fields are filled in, click **Save**.

Figure 5.2 Editing a contacts name

Adding Pictures to Contacts

If you are syncing your Google Contacts with your phone, then it is always nice to have your friend's picture on your contacts. Even if you are just browsing, a picture can more quickly find your friend than browsing names down a list.

By clicking on **Add a picture**, a pop up will appear asking you to browse your computer for a suitable picture. Remember to click **Save** when you are done.

You may notice from figure 5.3 that you can choose pictures from the web or Picasa or you can have no picture at all. To choose these options, don't click on browse next to the empty box instead click on the option you want under **My Computer**.

Figure 5.3 Adding a picture to a contact

If you want to change the picture later, hover your mouse over the existing image and click. You will get the option to change it.

Filling in the fields

Email, **Phone** and **Address** can all be customized. Once you add in your friend's email address, click out of the box and it will automatically save the address. By default Google will assign the email address as the **Home** address of the contact you are adding. To change this hover your mouse over **Home** and click on the drop down arrow that appears. You have a choice of **home**, **work** or **custom**. If you choose **custom** then when you have clicked on a blank piece of screen, a message to say **Type here** will show. Click on here and type in what the email is for. Home and work are the usual email address types but your friend could have two jobs or she could just have several email addresses. You can keep on adding email addresses by choosing **Add email** which appears under the email address you have entered.

Phone and address is similar, follow the same steps as above to customize these fields.

Under Address, Google gives you the option of adding birthdays. This can be changed to anniversary or any other special date by clicking custom.

If your contact has a website, put the address under URL. If this contact relates to work, this could your contact's company website.

Last but not least, there is a big box with Add a note to the right. This is invaluable for work or acquaintances. Add as much or as little information as you want here. This could be particularly useful if you can't remember when or where you met someone!

Note, by clicking on Groups you can organize your contacts. Google has suggested friends, family and colleagues but you can add more groups.

Why should you add groups? If you have hundreds of contacts in a long list, it can be time consuming to find the name you need. Of course you can search for them, but what if you can't remember how to spell their name or even what their name is?

You may for example have a group for Anycompany PLC. You know you want to talk to the director's PA but can't remember her name. With two thousand contacts (you are very popular), it would be impossible to find him/her just from browsing.

This is where Groups comes into its own. When you were putting your contacts from Anycompany PLC into your contacts you created a group of the same name. Now when you go in to your contacts, your groups will appear under My Contacts on the left hand side (under **NEW CONTACT**). You just click on Anycompany PLC and a list of contacts at that company will appear in the main window.

Of course you could also search for PA in the search window as long as you put his/her job title in their details.

You can have your contacts in more than one Group. For example your best friend may work for a certain company and you would want your friend in your Friends Group but also for example Anycompany PLC.

Figure 5.4 Adding a contact

Editing Contacts

To change the details on your contacts, simply click on the information you want to change and it becomes editable. Change it and click on **Save now**.

Chapter 6 Sorting emails – No more folders

Google is second to none as a tool for organizing emails. There are four big guns in the Google arsenal. These are discussions (mentioned in detail in Chapter Three), Labels, Filters and Spam protection.

Labels

Labels are what folders were in other programs and that antiquated filing cabinet gathering dust in the corner of your garage (because of course you have a paperless home office now). I used to have folders for everything including folders within folders. I had folders for holidays, work, friends, shopping, advice and many more. The old way *was* organized but there was always a point where you had to make a choice of where something went in your folder structure. For example if I planned a holiday with my friend to go shopping. Which folder would it go under? I would have chosen holidays in the past. Probably narrowing it down to Holidays > New York or something to that effect.

With Google Mail (Gmail) you don't have to make a choice, create the labels and add them all to the one email. If I look in any of the

Holidays, New York, Friends or Shopping labels I can now find it easily and quickly. Simply put, you can label your emails with as many 'labels' as you want. Whatever makes it easier to find the information you need.

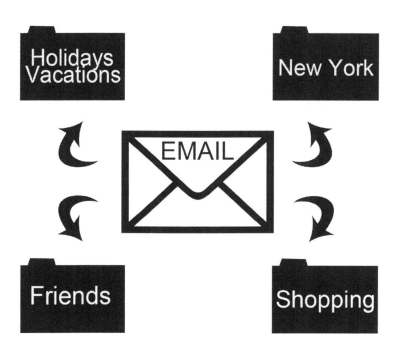

Figure 6.1 Labels

Creating a Label

Making a label is simple. Click on the gear symbol at the top right of the webpage (when you hover your mouse over the gear wheel it should confirm that it is the settings function). A drop down menu will appear - you will need to select **Settings**. The reason you have to select it twice is that Google has put a few extra cosmetic options which they feel you might need to see first, such as how compact you would like the webpage to appear. Click on **Labels** as in figure

6.2. Scroll down the page, past **System Labels** and you will see just **Labels** as in the section labeled number 2 in figure 6.2:

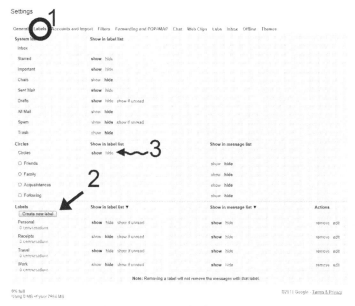

Figure 6.2 Labels screen

Click on **Create new label** as seen above (the arrow marked 2). Type in the box the label name you want, for example **Shopping** and think about if you want it to be a nested label.

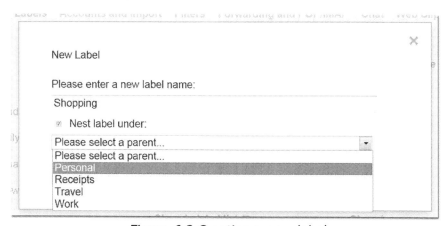

Figure 6.3 Creating a new label

A nested label means that a label will appear under another in the label list as in the following image:

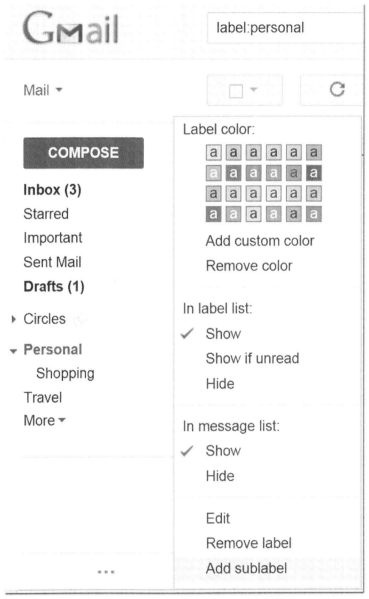

Figure 6.4 Labels in navigation bar

Shopping now appears under **Personal**. If you click on the little arrow to the left of the **Personal** label, you can hide the **Shopping** label and any other you have 'nested' under **Personal**.

I would like to sound a note of warning about the use of nested labels. If you label an email with **Shopping**, even though it will be under **Personal** in the list, the email will not appear if you click on **Personal**. Therefore if you want it to be available under the two labels then you must make sure that both labels are selected on an email if you want that email to appear when you look under each label.

Click **Create** once you have chosen if you want the label to be nested or not.

Your new label will then appear in the list of labels below the box.

All the labels can be customized further. There is a little arrow to the right of each label in the navigation section. Once you click on this a menu will appear with these options. See figure 6.4.

A particular useful feature is you can change the color of the labels. For example if you have an urgent label, you could color it red. If your favorite color is blue why not make your Friends label blue?

Circles

This is an option within the Labels settings page. I personally like to keep my Google+ Circles separate from my Gmail. I have made many friends on Google+ but they are not close friends which I would necessarily want to email. That is what Google+ is for – to communicate with friends and acquaintances across the world. If I was particularly close with someone in my circles I would move them over into my main contacts.

Therefore my recommendation is to hide Circles from your Gmail account. As illustrated in figure 6.3, click on hide (pointed to by the wavy arrow labeled number 3), the Circles should then disappear from your Gmail homepage.

Applying a Label

Now that you have created a Label you will want to add it to your email.

From the email list

Check the box on the left of the email that you would like to label. Once you have done this, options for organizing your emails will appear above the email list. Choose the icon (picture) that looks like a luggage label as illustrated in figure 6.6 by clicking on the little arrow to the right of the icon.

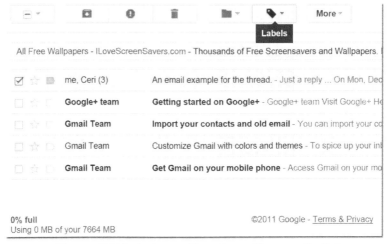

Figure 6.5 Labels position from the emails list

A dropdown list will appear.

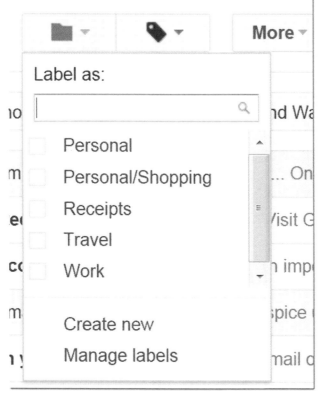

Figure 6.6 Label options when applying labels

Tick the bock next to the label you want, you can choose as many as you like. If you have too many labels to appear in the list you can save time by searching for the labels by typing a few characters in the search box. You don't need to search for the whole word. **Create new** at the bottom of the list will do exactly as the name suggests and will allow you to create a new label. By clicking on **Manage labels** you will be taken to the Labels page in the settings area of Gmail.

From an opened email

The options are similar to applying labels from the list of emails in the Gmail homepage. Choose the luggage tag icon to the right of the options as in figure 6.8.

Figure 6.7 Applying labels from an opened email

At this point you can assign as many Labels as you want to it. Once you click **Apply**, the email will be assigned or 'moved' to the Label 'folder'.

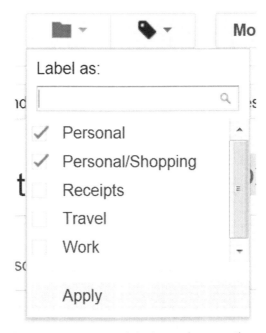

Figure 6.8 Assign as many labels to the email as you want

To remove a Label, click on the X next to the Label. This can be seen in figure 6.10 below in the subject box.

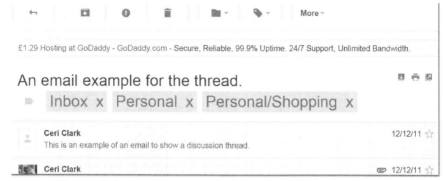

Figure 6.9 Click the X to remove the labels from emails

You can see what else is labeled by looking at the top of the opened email.

Filters

Applying Labels to everything can be a bit of a chore; however Google has come up with an elegant solution with *Filters*.

Filters allow you to automate the process of adding Labels. With this system, if you always want to put all emails from Auntie Flo in a Label called Auntie Flo, then you can get Filters to do this, you can also ask it to treat the emails as very important. It might not mean that you answer her emails any faster but will mean that you won't lose her email amongst the hundreds of other emails you get, ...or lose it in the spam folder.

Creating a Filter

Go to **Settings** on the top right of the screen and choose settings from the dropdown then **Filters**.

Click on **Create a new filter**.

Ceri Clark

General   Labels   Accounts and Import   **Filters**   Forwarding and POP/IMAP   Chat   Web Clips

The following filters are applied to all incoming mail:

Create a new filter

Figure 6.10 Creating a filter

Options will appear as shown in figure 6.13.

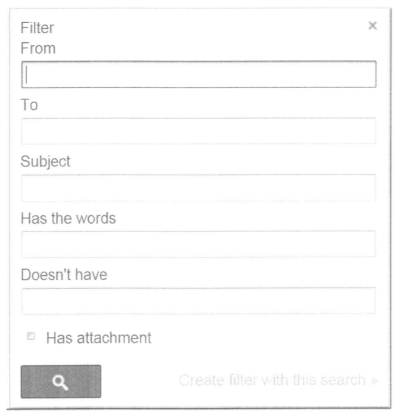

Figure 6.11 Filter options

Examples of how to filter:

- To label all emails from a person or mailing list, type the email address into the **From** box. For example, auntieflo@gmail.com.

- If there are specific words in the subject you want to pay attention to, for example if you receive a newsletter from horse riding weekly and you want to make sure they all appear together in one place then put horse riding weekly into the **Subject** box.

- **Has the words** are for general keywords, for example any emails containing your family's names.

- The **Doesn't have** is a powerful tool. If you want to label all emails with a word but you are getting too many results and all these wrong results have the same word in them. Pop that word into this box and it will ignore those emails with the wrong word in them.

- **Has attachment.** If you want all emails with attachments from a certain person to go in the **Bin** then, type in the person's name in the **From** box and click the box by **Has attachment** and you will never receive the emails again.

Remember you can use one of the filter options or all. You are only limited by your imagination. Once you have put the words you want to put in the filter, click on Search to see if there are any emails already in your account with these options. If there are, choose **Also apply filter to (?) matching results**. This will tidy your inbox as well as organize future emails. Once you are happy with your selections click on **Create filter with this search**.

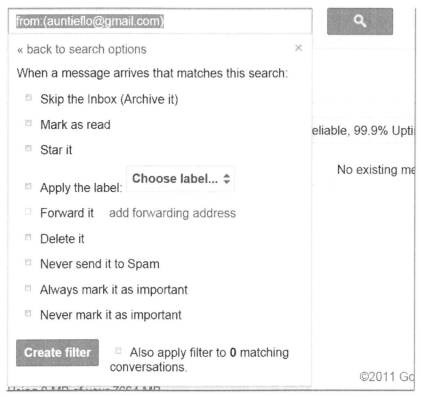

Figure 6.12 The next step in creating a filter

Figure 6.12 shows the next options available to you. You can archive it, mark it as read, star it, apply the label, and forward those particular emails to an email address and so on.

The most important options are **Apply the Label** and **Always/Never mark it as important**.

After clicking on **Create Filter**, you will get a confirmation screen to say it has been set up. The downside is that you will have to go through the process for each label as it doesn't allow you to choose more than one label at this stage.

Spam

As you may know Spam is the bane of all email users everywhere. Unwanted emails about medical aids, Nigerian princes needing help to take money from you or fake bank emails bring misery to billions. Fortunately Google has one of the best spam filters on the web.

To find emails which may have been erroneously labeled spam, click on **Spam** on the left of the screen in the navigation bar and then relabel it.

One of the reasons that Google is so good with Spam is that there is a community effort to reduce it. Click on this symbol, ❗ above your emails to let Google know the current email you are reading is spam. Spam is unsolicited bulk email, it may or may not be malicious, it can just be annoying.

There is another type of email which is sent with the sole intent to cause either harm or take money from you. If you receive an email which you think is trying to trick you to going to a fake bank website that has 'slipped through the net', click on **Report phishing** in the menu that appears when you click on the arrow at the top right of each email (see number 1 in figure 5.13 for the location). Number 2 in the same image shows where to report.

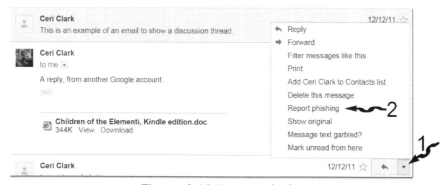

Figure 6.13 Report phishing

Ceri Clark

If you archive emails, you can always find them later in **All Mail.**

Chapter 7 Searching for emails

Searching for your emails is a breeze with Gmail. Type in your search term and then click on the magnifying glass, the Google engine will then search all your email for you.

Figure 7.1 Search Google mail

Google does accept Boolean searching, for example using AND & OR, and quotes, but for a simple way of more powerful searching click on the little arrow on the right inside the search box. You will get the option to click on **Show search options**. Do this and the following screen will appear:

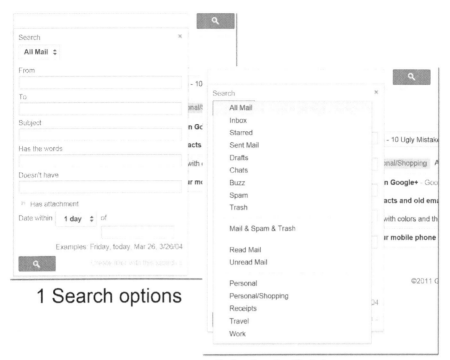

1 Search options

2 Labels/folders you can limit your search to.

Figure 7.2 Advanced search options

The beauty of these options is that you can not only search from a particular email address but from emails which have certain words in them.

My best advice is to use the advanced options and to use whole words if possible. At the time of writing, a search was tested using part-words and wildcards (*) but the search was unsuccessful, even though there was an email with the words I was testing in there. This may be possible in the future but for now using the advanced search is your best option.

Chapter 8 Changing the look and feel

You've sent a couple of emails, told a few of your best mates about how great Gmail is but you're getting a bit bored with how it looks and you want one of those cool signatures! This is the chapter to help you with this.

All of these changes can be made from **Settings**. This link can be found at the top right of the screen as illustrated in figure 8.1.

Figure 8.1 Where to find settings

Density Display

First of all there are three options under Display Density. Comfortable, Cozy and Compact. Please see figure 7.2 to see each view side-by-side for comparison. They are designed to fit more or less email depending on the size of the screen you are viewing your email on.

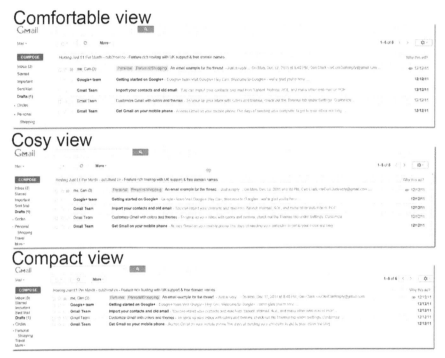

Figure 8.2 Density views

Themes

To change the theme, choose the themes option under settings under the gear wheel at the top right of the page. The themes can also be found as an option at the top of the settings page.

There are lots of themes to choose from and quite a few change throughout the day, my particular favorite is the planets theme.

You can also add custom themes by uploading your pictures. Choose light or dark depending on your picture and upload when prompted.

Figure 8.3 Themes available

General Settings

The number of general settings can seem quite daunting when you first see them. This section aims to dispel the horror of all those settings in one page.

Figure 8.4 General settings

Language

Choose the language appropriate to your region, for the US, this is the default, while UK users can choose the English (UK) option.

Maximum Page Size

This option depends on how much you want to scroll, the more conversations and contacts you allow on each page the fewer pages you will have to click through but it also means you will have to scroll more (and it may take slightly longer to load).

Keyboard Shortcuts

Turn these on or off depending on how much you want to use your mouse. I would recommend this is turned on so that you have the option to use shortcuts if you want to. A selection of shortcuts taken from the Google help pages are:

To compose a message: "<Shift> + c "

To return to the inbox type "u"

To archive a message, type "e"

To report spam, type "!"

To bring up the label menu, type "l" (lowercase L)

To undo an action (it might not *always* work), type "z"

For all Google Gmail shortcuts, visit the Google help page at: http://support.google.com/mail/bin/answer.py?answer=6594

External Content

This refers to displaying images within emails. While it is nice to see adverts in all their glory, if an email slips through which has harmful code in it, it could damage your computer. It is best to click on **Ask**

before displaying external content. If this drives you up the wall, you can always change to the other option again later.

Browser Connection

Choosing **Always use https** is the safer option but may cause problems when using your mobile to view this. Again this can always be changed later.

Conversation view

You can turn this off or on here. I would recommend you keep this on as it means you keep all your email about one 'subject' in one place.

Stars

Stars are used to help organize your email. For example if you star an important email that you need to deal with by next week, then you can search for just starred email. Use this section to choose what stars will be available. Drag the stars and symbols from the **Not in use** row to the **In use** row and click **Save changes** at the bottom of the page. To choose a different star, in your inbox click on the star symbol next to the email in the inbox. Keep clicking to get the different star and symbol options.

Desktop Notifications

If you are using Google's Chrome browser, then you can get notifications like popups to let you know when you have got new email. It doesn't work on other browsers at the time of writing.

My Picture

In this section you can change the picture you selected during setup. Clicking on **Change Picture** brings up a window where you can search your computer for your favorite pic of yourself. You can always use your cat's picture if you prefer! Remember you can control who can see your picture, whether just people who chat with you or who email you once you have uploaded the picture. For example:

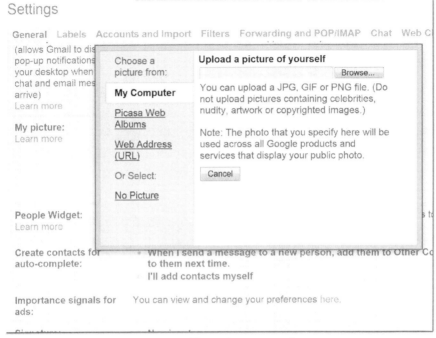

Figure 8.5 Changing your picture

For more in-depth guidance on adding/changing your picture, please refer to the **Adding your profile picture** in Chapter 1.

People Widget

This shows information about your contacts next to your emails, usually at the top right when you are in an open email.

Create contacts for auto-complete

This is a great time saver. Instead of adding contacts manually, Gmail will add them automatically when you send an email to someone. Of course if you send a lot of emails to people you are sure that you never want to contact again then using the **I'll add contacts myself** option would be better.

Signature

Your signature is how you end your email, it saves you having to type the same information time and time again. You can just add text, your name, address, phone number etc., or you can add images.

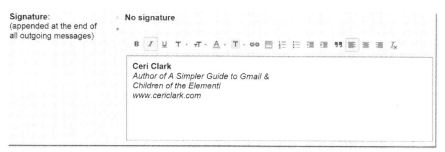

Figure 8.6 Adding a signature

To add an image to your email signature using Picasa

You can add an image from any publicly available online storage simply by typing the location of the image in the box provided. However, Google's Picasa is the logical choice if you do not already have storage, after all your profile picture you uploaded earlier is on there already and by opening any Google account you will automatically have a Picasa account.

What is Picasa? Picasa is free online storage of photos and images. You can download software from Picasa http://picasa.google.com which will help you organise your photos on your computer. However for the purposes of the email signature the online uploading feature is the one you need.

Point your browser to https://picasaweb.google.com/home by typing this in your address bar of your favourite browser. Login with the same username and password as your Gmail account. You will find your profile picture already stored here.

Ceri Clark

First click on upload (as seen on the top right of the first image in figure 8.6).

Figure 8.7 Uploading pictures to Picasa

The second picture will load. Click on **Select photos from your computer**. From here you can browse the file on your computer to find the picture you want. Click on it and it will upload in the window, replacing the **Select photos from your computer**. You can change the Album name before or after this step. I have chosen Email Signatures as seen in the above figure. Click **OK**.

Next you need to link to the signature. Find the picture in your new album and click on the image. You will be taken to a page with the image on and some options on the right. Click on **link to this photo** under tags (as seen in the next figure).

Figure 8.8 Getting the link for the uploaded photo

Do not choose the **Link** box as this links to the page not the image. What you need to do is select the checkbox **Image only (no link)**. I know this sounds counterintuitive but bear with me. The **Embed image** box will now have a direct link to the picture. Highlight the text in this box and right-click on it (or cmd-click on Mac) then choose **Copy**.

Next go back to your Gmail account, click on the gear wheel, then settings. Making sure that you are in the general settings, scroll down to the signature section.

Next make sure that you have clicked the little circle next to the signature box and then the insert image icon on the formatting bar.

If you hover your mouse over each icon (small picture) then text will appear telling you what it is.

Place your curser into the box next to **image URL** in the window that loads. Either press **ctrl** and **v** at the same time on your keyboard to paste the address that you saved from Picasa or right click and choose Paste (cmd+v or cmd+click on Macs). Your image will automatically load as demonstrated in the next figure.

If the picture doesn't appear at first make sure the folder you created in Picasa is public.

Figure 8.9 Inserting the image address into the signature

Click **OK**. Remember to click save on the settings page (located at the bottom).

The next time you want to email someone when you click on **Compose,** your image will automatically appear in the email ready.

Figure 8.10 email signature in Compose

Personal level indicators

I would recommend turning these on, but if you don't plan on joining any mailing lists, then this is not important. This could be a good indicator of spam. You would find out if the email was sent directly to you and not to a generic mailing list address before you opened it.

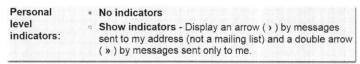

Figure 8.11 Personal Level indicators

Snippets

This option is a matter of personal preference. If you check your email in a public place then you may prefer to have this switched off. What it does is put the first line of your email viewable from the inbox. It can be a time saver as it tells you what is new in a conversation at first glance but it can also let other people looking over your shoulder know a little of what has been sent to you. The choice is yours.

Out of Office AutoReply

This section is very useful in a business context. It allows you to tell your contacts that you are not available when you are on holiday or if you are indisposed. If you want to use this for your holidays, remember to click on **Only send a response to people in my Contacts**. You don't want potential burglars knowing you are on holiday!

You can schedule the message so it will be sent while you are away and automatically turn off when you are back.

Another possible (business) use of this is as an autoresponder could be if you were to not include an end date. You can write a message such as "Thank you for your email. Your message is important to us and we will get back to you as soon as possible."

Again you can restrict this message to people in your contacts if you put phone numbers and other contact details in your signature or autoreply message that you may not want generally known.

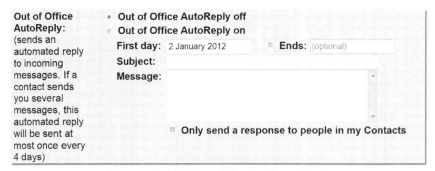

Figure 8.12 Out of Office AutoReply

Outgoing message encoding

Keep this as the option already chosen.

Attachments

I would recommend keeping the default option but be aware that if you are using this option you may not be able to attach files as Flash is required. As Google enhances Gmail over time this requirement is likely to change though. If you have an Android phone this of course does not apply as Flash is available on these phones anyway.

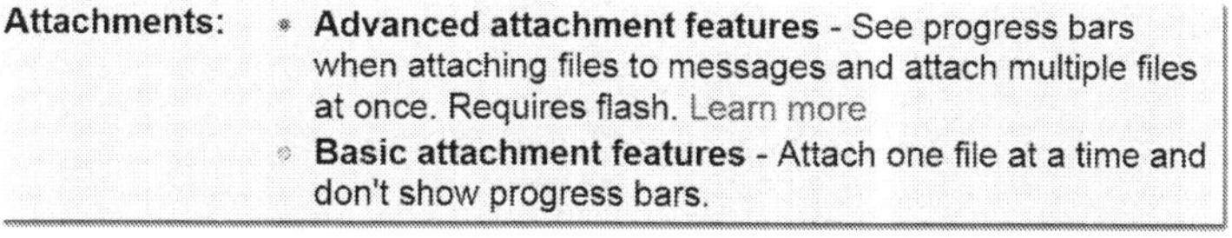

Attachments: * **Advanced attachment features** - See progress bars when attaching files to messages and attach multiple files at once. Requires flash. Learn more
* **Basic attachment features** - Attach one file at a time and don't show progress bars.

Figure 8.13 Attachment settings

Remember to click on **Save Changes**!

Labels

I have gone into more depth in Chapter Five: Sorting emails – No more folders, but if you have jumped to this section, basically, think of them as folders but where one email can be in several folders/places at the same time.

This is the place where you can specify what labels i.e. 'folders' you want to see on the left column. I would suggest you need the Sent Mail, Drafts, All Mail and Bin and anything else when and as you need it.

Accounts and Import

This section is for importing your old email from another provider. If you have never had an email address before or you just want a separate email address, you can skip most of this section.

Figure 8.14 Accounts and import settings

Most of these options are self-explanatory or lead to wizards which will help you with the set up.

You may have several email addresses which you may want to keep but only wish to send email from one place. This can be done in the **Accounts and Import** section under **Send mail as**. This will mean that you can choose to send from email addresses you already have access to, which will make the recipient think you sent it from somewhere else. It also means that all your sent email will be in the one place for ease of searching.

As you would expect the email address you just created is already there. To add another one, click on **Add another email address you own**. A popup will appear giving you a wizard to follow:

1. Enter your name and email address that you already own or have permission to access.

2. Decide whether to keep the **Treat as alias** ticked or not. Untick if you are emailing on someone else's behalf and you want replies to go their inbox and not yours).

3. For ease of setup, choose **Send through Gmail servers**, instead of your other provider's.

4. Verify your email address. Click **Send verification**. Google does not want unauthorized people sending from other accounts. It also ensures that if someone tried to do this for *your* account without you knowing you are notified that someone is trying to access it. You or the person you are allowing access to your account will receive an email checking to see if they are OK with this. They or you need to click the confirmation link in the email address. If there is a problem with the link, there is a verification code as well. The easiest way by far is to click the link though.

5. Close the window and you will see that your new email address now appears in the settings with **unverified**, **verify** and **delete.** It is of course unverified until the confirmation link is clicked, verify will send you another verification email and by clicking delete you remove the email address from the account.

6. Once you have verified the access, log back in to your account. If you go back to your **Accounts and Import** section in the settings you will see that the previous options of **unverified**, **verify** and **delete** have been replaced with **make default**, **edit info** and **delete**. Only click on **Make default** if you want this to be your primary address, the one that you want to receive and send emails with. Otherwise you will get the option of which email you want to use each time you compose an email.

7. Make sure under the **When replying to a message** that you choose the **Reply from the same address to which the message was sent**. Otherwise, life can get very confusing for you and your recipient. They won't know where they should be emailing and you may give out an email address you wouldn't want a stranger, for example, to know about.

You are now set up. When you next compose a message in the **From** field where your email address appears, you can now select the new address, if you so wish, simply by selecting the little arrow to the right of the email address.

Also in this section, you are given the option of using POP3 email. I would not recommend this. I would say import your emails and contacts and either use your new email address as is, or use the **Send mail as** feature through Gmail.

Using POP3 to import email means that you can import the email from the email address you have just created or from another address to this one on a regular basis but all folders won't be the same in every device you use. If you send from a different device then the emails from that device won't be replicated in your webmail account for example.

IMAP is a better solution which means there is a two way communication between the locations. Instead of just having your email 'pushed' to your new address, with IMAP your sent and received emails will be synchronized. This means if you are using IMAP and you are using Outlook to send emails, the emails you send will be on the web version of Gmail and also on your Android/Apple phones (if you use them). This is harder but not difficult to set up but you may as well just use Gmail on the web for convenience if you don't want to use IMAP or POP3.

Google does ask if you are using Gmail for work and refer you to their apps accounts. They do not guarantee anything with a free account. After all it is free and they are running a business. If you want more 'protection' then a paid apps system may be the way to go. Gmail can be sufficient for sole traders but you would need to read the terms and conditions of use to make a fully informed decision of what service you want to use.

Another interesting and useful feature is the **Grant Access to your Account**. This should only be done where there is the utmost trust involved but if you have a family member who doesn't really use email but they still need an account then this is a great way to help them. Another possible use is if you are a couple and want to use one account for accessing services. Instead of setting up forwarding for the emails sent by your electricity supplier why not have a joint account which you both have access to? You can of course remove access by a click of a button if you need to.

Filters

Please see Chapter Five: Sorting emails – No more folders for more information on this.

Figure 8.15 Filter settings

Forwarding and POP/IMAP

It is possible to forward all your email to another email address. For example if you would like your email to be forwarded to your work email address, then this is the place to do it.

Figure 8.16 Forwarding and POP/IMAP settings

You can forward specific emails by using filters instead of forwarding all your emails. For example you might find this useful if you want to forward copies of all emails from a utilities company to your partner/spouse.

Forwarding

To add a forwarding address, click on the grey box with the words **Add a forwarding address**. A pop up will appear asking you to add an address, type it in and then click **Next**.

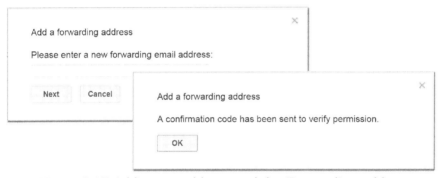

Figure 8.17 Adding an address and the Forwarding address confirmation screen

Click **OK** and then go to the email account you specified. Click on the link in the email sent to you from Gmail. A confirmation in a browser window will let you know you have been successful.

POP Download

POP mail is used for downloading into a desktop application such as Outlook. As this is a new email account, enabling POP for all mail if you want to use Outlook or another desktop client is a good option.

I would also recommend Archiving Gmail's copy in the drop down box. This means that when you visit the web version of Gmail you won't be overwhelmed with new email. You will know that if it has been downloaded it won't be in the inbox.

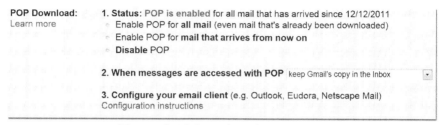

Figure 8.18 Pop download options

IMAP Access

This is recommended over POP as instead of simply downloading your emails you can interact and sync it with all your devices that access email, for example, both your desktop application such as Outlook and the web version of Gmail. This means that if you move an email in Outlook to a folder it will appear labeled in Gmail as well as other ways of accessing your email and vice-versa.

> **IMAP Access:**
> (access Gmail from other clients using IMAP)
> Learn more
>
> **Status: IMAP is disabled**
> ○ Enable IMAP
> ● Disable IMAP
>
> **Configure your email client** (e.g. Outlook, Thunderbird, iPhone)
> Configuration instructions

Figure 8.19 IMAP Access options

Make sure IMAP is enabled by clicking **Enable IMAP** and then remember to save any changes you've made.

The key settings to remember for setting up your IMAP access on your device is **imap.gmail.com** using port **993** (with SSL) for the incoming server and the outgoing server should be **smtp.gmail.com** on port **587** (with SSL).

If you are using an apps account, then you will need the same settings. The device you are using may try to use the domain from the email but ignore this and put the Gmail information in. For example don't let it put in imap.yourdomain.com, it should be imap.gmail.com.

Chat

If you enable this option then I would recommend keeping the options as they are. The only changes I would recommend would be to change the Auto-add suggested contacts to **Only allow people that I've explicitly approved to chat with me and see when I'm online**.

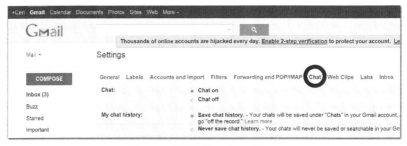

Figure 8.20 Chat settings

Web Clips

Web Clips are targeted ads, tips and other content Google feels you may be interested in. You have the option of turning them off by *un*ticking the check-box labeled **Show my web clips above the Inbox** at the top of the settings area. There used to be an option to keep webclips but remove certain subjects but this has been removed. I would recommend unchecking this box as there is already advertising in Gmail so if there is an opportunity to minimize advertising I would take it.

Labs

I would ignore this setting until you are completely familiar with the Gmail system. For more information on these, please see Chapter Fourteen: Advanced Features - Google Labs.

Inbox

You can customize how your inbox is organized here. The options are:

- Classic

- Important first

- Unread first

- Starred first

- Priority inbox

The classic inbox puts the newest emails at the top. Important first, unread first and starred first are all self-explanatory.

This leaves the Priority inbox. In this view items that Google think are most important will appear at the top. Click on **Priority inbox** next to the inbox type to activate it and then **Save Changes**.

Your inbox will instantly change as seen here:

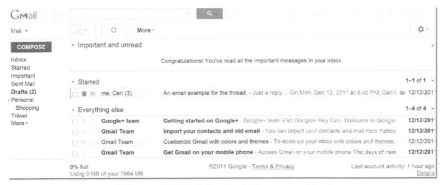

Figure 8.21 Priority inbox enabled

Your inbox can be customized further, once you have chosen the priority inbox you can choose how it is laid out with the following options:

Inbox sections:		
	1. **Important and unread**	Options ▾
	2. **Starred**	Options ▾
	3. Empty	Add section ▾
	4. **Everything else**	Options ▾

Figure 8.22 Priority inbox sections

By clicking on **Options** you can change how many emails appear in each section but number 3 is the most interesting option of these. Click **Add Section** and you can choose a label as a section. This means that you can have all your emails about a certain subject right there in full view in your inbox. If you have set up filters so that your inbox is bypassed, you will see the newest five emails on the subject of your choice.

You can bypass filters by the **Filtered mail** section of the inbox settings. This will include emails that Google feels is important to you even if you have filtered them out.

Offline

Only enable this if you have an unsteady internet connection or none for periods of time.

Themes

Changing your theme is as simple as clicking on the picture you like. More detail can be found earlier in this Chapter.

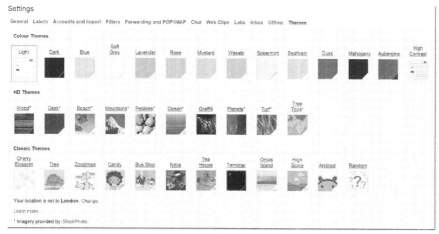

Figure 8.23 Themes available

Once saved your Gmail account will now always show the theme you have chosen (until you change it again of course). The screenshot below shows the Planets theme.

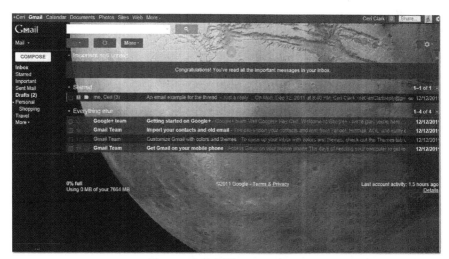

Figure 8.24 Planets theme

89

Ceri Clark

Chapter 9 Google Accounts and Your Profile

Gmail is one in a large family of products offered for free by Google. All of these services can be accessed using your Google Account and Profile. The same account for all the products means that you only need one username and password to use Gmail, Google Docs, iGoogle, Calendar etc. Who wants to remember hundreds of passwords? Note, you can go direct to these services from the top of Gmail as can be seen in figure 9.1.

Figure 9.1 How to find other Google services

You can put as much or as little information into your Google Profile. You only need to have a public profile if you intend to use Google+.

Ceri Clark

To modify your account or edit your public profile, you need to go to your settings, click on **Accounts and Import** and then choose **Other Google Account settings**.

Settings

General   Labels   **Accounts and Import**   Filters   Forwarding

Inbox   Offline   Themes

| **Change account settings:** | Change password
Change password recovery options
Other Google Account settings |

Figure 9.2 Edit Google account settings

A new window will appear with your Google Account Settings. You can also use this as a springboard to find other Google services.

Creating a Public Profile

You will need to have a public profile to use Google+. Once you are in your account page (follow the instructions at the beginning of this chapter), click on **Edit profile** as seen in Figure 9.3.

Figure 9.3 Edit your profile

You will be taken to the Editing your Profile page:

Figure 9.4 Editing your profile page

Once you have filled in all the fields that you want to, click on **Done editing** at the top of the screen.

Adding as much information as possible can make it easier for your friends to find you but consider how much information you are comfortable with sharing with the world.

Ceri Clark

Chapter 10 Introduction to Google+

Google+ is a growing social network. It is a cross between Facebook and Twitter with the advantages of both and a higher attention to privacy issues.

Now that you have a Google Account you will automatically have a Google+ account. To login, simply find your name on the top left of the screen when you are logged in to any Google service and click on your name. There is usually a + before your name. For example, my account says +Ceri. If it says +You, then you are not logged in to Google.

On the left of the screen is the main navigation bar, which looks like this:

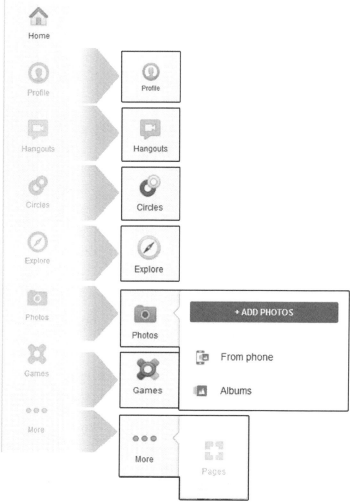

Figure 10.1 Google+ navigation

When you hover your mouse over the left navigation bar, the pictures become colored and clearer as seen in the graphic above.

Home (The Stream)

Yours and everyone's posts from people in your circles will appear in the stream. These can range from text only, to links, photos and videos.

You can limit posts by clicking on the small navigation bar above the stream. This looks like this.

If you can't find the circle that you created, click on **More** and all your circles will appear in a drop down bar.

Profile

Find all your own posts here. You can also edit your public profile viewable from Google+.

A nice feature is that just above your posts on the right hand side, **under View as**..., you can see how your profile looks to a group or a particular person. If you have a different persona for work and home this is particularly useful.

Hangouts

This is my favorite feature of Google+. Why restrict yourself to chatting by video to one person at a time? Google Hangout lets you talk to up to 9 people at the same time from anywhere as long as everyone has an internet connection and installed the plugin.

I personally have had conversations with people from the United States, UK and Canada all at the same time. This is great for book groups and keeping in touch with family.

Google Hangouts are, simply put, for group video chats. You can chat one-to-one but the fun is in having lots of people chatting together (maximum of nine). It is a free service and very easy to use, simply click on Hangout on the left navigation bar and then click on **Start a Hangout** on the top right of the screen, allow the plugin to be installed if you haven't already done so and wait for people to join you.

When you start a hangout you can broadcast that you have started one to circles or individuals. It will appear in their streams that you are LIVE and they can join you from there.

You can also invite people from inside the Hangout by clicking on **Invite** on the top left of the screen. You can text chat if someone is having problems with their microphone and watch a YouTube video while you are waiting for people to join you. If you want to really be wacky, try the Google effects for Google to put funny faces on you while you chat!

Other options on the top right of the screen are **Mute the video** (if you have a camera shy partner or friend who needs to come in the room), **Mute the Mic** (should you wish to shout at your partner down the stairs for a cup of tea), **Settings** and **Exit**.

Reasons to use Hangouts

Distance family get-togethers

Book Clubs

Watching sports/films/TV shows with friends

Classes

Meetings

Google+ Posting Cheat Sheet

Text Styling

Example starring text will bold the words and it will look like **Example**.

Example underscoring text will italicise the words and it will look like *Example*.

-Example- hyphenating on either side of text will strike out the text so it will look like ~~Example~~.

Posting

Add + or @ to mention people in your posts.

Prevent re-sharing of your posts by clicking the arrow at the top right of each post and clicking 'Disable reshare'.

Shortcut keys

Pressing Space will scroll down the page.

J will scroll down one post at a time

K will scroll up one post at a time.

Press Return to start a comment

Tab, Return to end a comment and

Q will go to chat.

Circles

At the heart of Google+ is the Circles system. These are groups of people that you have to set up. They are private and no one knows what you call your Circles – only that they are *in* one of your circles.

The sky is the limit for how many Circles you have or what you want to name them. There is however a limit of just over 5,000 people that you can add. You can be put in any number of other people's Circles.

You don't have to add people who add you and vice-versa, you can block people, talk to individual people or have public posts to have conversations with hundreds of people. Unlike Twitter, all the elements are in one place so you can follow a conversation easily and get notified when something new is said.

Remember whenever you post you have to post to a Circle or particular person. You have complete control over who you want to see what you say. This is very useful for keeping family and friends informed without everyone else knowing what you post. Just don't post everything to public unless you want everyone and his dog to see it. This is fine for the most part but bear in mind that future employers may have a quick look at your profile to see what you are like.

Adding people to your Circles

When you first login, Google will put you through a tutorial where you can add contacts from your email accounts. It uses the email addresses in your contacts to find them within the Google+ system. If you skip this it will then ask if you want to add people that you have contacted through your email. If you have emailed friends or family this is an easy introduction to adding someone to a Circle.

On the picture of the contact Google is suggesting click and drag the picture down to a circle on the lower half of the screen. You now have your first person in a Circle. If there are no Circles suitable drop the picture into the first Circle with the words **Drop here to create a circle**.

The tutorial will continue, suggesting people that you may be interested in, finishing by asking for personal information. Don't feel that you have to fill in all the information. Only put in what you are comfortable with allowing people to know.

You can also search for people by name. For example I searched for the author Alison DeLuca and added her to my circle called 'authors'.

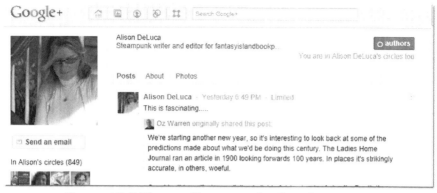

Figure 10.2 The profile page of a Google+ contact

Creating a Circle

Go to the little picture of overlapping circles on the left of the screen.

Figure 10.3 Circles icon

Find a work Colleague by searching for their name. If they are on there, their name should appear on the screen. Clicking on this will take you to their profile. There is a bright orange button which says **Add to circles**. Hover the mouse over this button and you will be given the option of adding them to your circles. You can choose a category already there or click on **create a circle.** Type in the box the name of the circle you want (your contact will not know what Circle they are in) and the option will then appear pre-ticked. The next time you hover your mouse over the contact you will see what circles they are in.

Go back to the Circles page by clicking the little icon on the left navigation bar again. You will see your newly created circle in the bottom half of the screen with the number of people in it. If there is one circle that you use more than any other you can reorder the circles to put the one you use the most on the left.

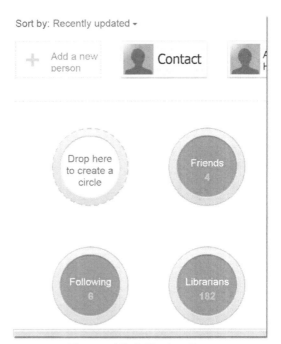

Sort by: Recently updated ▾

Add a new person

Contact

Drop here to create a circle

Friends
4

Following
6

Librarians
182

Figure 10.4 Circles Page

You can make your contacts or circles section bigger on the Circles page by 'grabbing' the line between the two and dragging up or down.

You can add more people by looking at Google's suggestions. The more people that you add from your own contacts, the better Google is able to suggest other people they think you will be interested in based on their profile information.

To remove someone from your circles, hover your mouse over their picture in the Circles page and click on the X which appears on the top right of the box their profile picture is in.

A good tip to know is to create a Circle with no people in it called Bookmarks. If you found any posts that you think are particularly interesting or useful you can share them with this empty Circle. This then becomes your personal folder that no one has access to but you.

To view posts by a particular group of people, click on the Circle at the top of the screen in Stream view (Home). You will only see posts by people in that particular group.

Photos

This is where all the photos you upload can be seen. These are not stored in Google+ but in Picasa but you can choose how they are visible on Google+ and who can see them from individuals to Circles (groups of people).

Games

Facebook has had great success with social gaming. This is where you can find online social games on Google+.

Posting

Posting on Google+ is as easy as Facebook or Twitter so if you are familiar with these services you already have a head start. Click on the Home icon as shown in the beginning of this chapter, and start typing your post in the box immediately below the navigation bar under Stream.

You have four options once you have put in some text, you can add a photo, insert a video, add a link or put in your location by choosing the icons underneath the text box. Once you are done you can choose who will see your post. By default your first post will be set to be **Public** which will mean anyone will be able to see what you have said. To remove this, click in the box and press delete. A dropdown of all your options will appear. You can choose one of your Circles (groups) to see your post or you can start typing someone's name in if you only want a certain person to see it. Once you are happy with your post, click **Share** and it will be live. To see how it looks, go to your profile and your latest post will always be the top post.

Viewing Posts

You can see all the posts from people in your circles in your Stream.

You can see posts by people not in your circle by clicking on their photo and looking in their stream. If they have allowed you to view their posts, you will be able to see them.

If you want to serendipitously stumble upon an interesting post click on **Explore** on the left to find what Google thinks you might be interested in.

Notifications

Sometimes you just don't have time to go through your stream but notifications allows you to know if anyone has commented on posts you have created, if there has been any comments on posts you have commented on and who has added you on Google+.

You can remove certain types of notifications by clicking ignore. For example I did this for gaming notifications. After receiving a hundred requests for the lost mystical sword of Zorg for someone's game, I was getting a little frustrated. Luckily Google allows you to customise what notifications you receive.

Chapter 11 Chat

To turn on Chat follow the instructions in Chapter Two: Getting Started. The Chat function can be found in the left navigation bar. You will need to invite someone to chat in the first instance but after that, your contact will be in the chat list.

Type your contacts email address in the white box under Chat as seen in figure 11.1. Google will look through your contacts and find the contact for you, giving you the following options:

Figure 11.1 Inviting contacts to chat

A message will be sent to your contact asking them to accept you as a potential chat partner.

Remember to set your status so your friends can contact you.

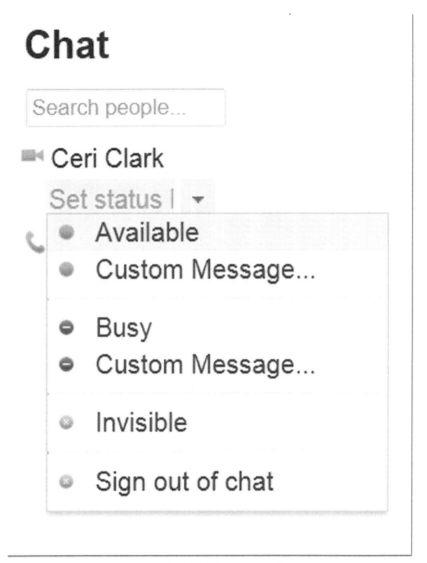

Figure 11.2 Setting your status

An example of a chat window in operation is shown in the next figure:

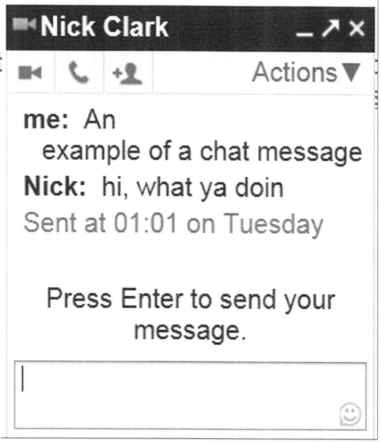

Figure 11.3 The chat window

By clicking on the little slanting arrow in the black bar, you can pop out the chat window from your Gmail account. Don't close your Gmail page though as this can lead to the Chat window closing as well. To start a video chat (as long as you have a webcam) click on the video camera icon just underneath the black bar. If you click on the phone icon, then you can have a voice only chat with contacts.

The actions button gives you the option of typing off the record so it doesn't get recorded in your email and also the option of blocking the person you are chatting to, particularly useful for ex-boyfriends/girlfriends.

Ceri Clark

Chapter 12 Tasks

Tasks are a great way of remembering lists of things to do. As long as you have access to the internet you can add, edit and delete from your task list wherever you are. Whether on your smartphone or on your computer at home, use tasks to organize your life.

Where to find Tasks

Tasks can be found on the left navigation bar in the top left corner of your screen as seen in Figure 10.1.

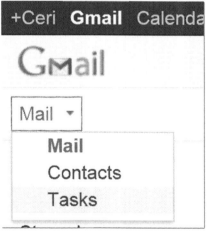

Figure 12.1 Where to find tasks

Ceri Clark

By clicking on Tasks a popup will appear on the bottom right of the screen which looks like this:

Figure 12.2 Tasks window explained

The buttons on the top of the task window do three things:

a minimizes the window

b pops the window to a larger, new browser window

c Closes the Task window completely

Adding a task

To add a task, right click next to the little white box and start typing. After you've made the first task you can then click on the + button at the bottom of each window to make another.

If you want to add more details to a task (such as a due date) click on the arrow pointing right, on the line of the subject and the page in figure 12.3 will load:

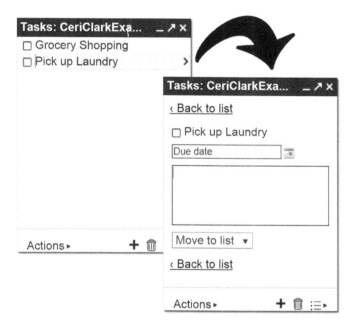

Figure 12.3 Adding details to a task

Click on **Back to List**, and the main tasks window will appear again. All the information is then displayed under the task subject. There is no need to save, Google will automatically do this for you.

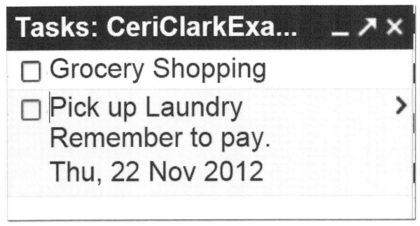

Figure 12.4 Example of a tasks list

Completing a task

To complete a task simply check the box next to the subject. The text will have a line through it so you know you've done it.

Deleting or removing a task

To remove a task, click on the subject and click on the trash can (bin) symbol at the bottom of the task window.

Actions

Clicking on **Actions** as seen in figure 12.5 can give you more options.

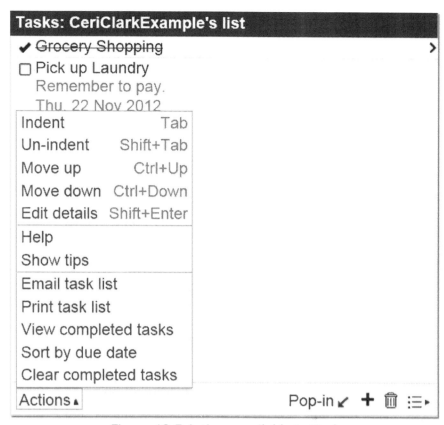

Figure 12.5 Actions available in Tasks

Indent and Unindent

These options will allow you to move dependent tasks in as if you had a tab command in a word processor. Click on the subject, then **Actions**, then **Indent**. The subject will then move. For an example of how this might work see the next figure.

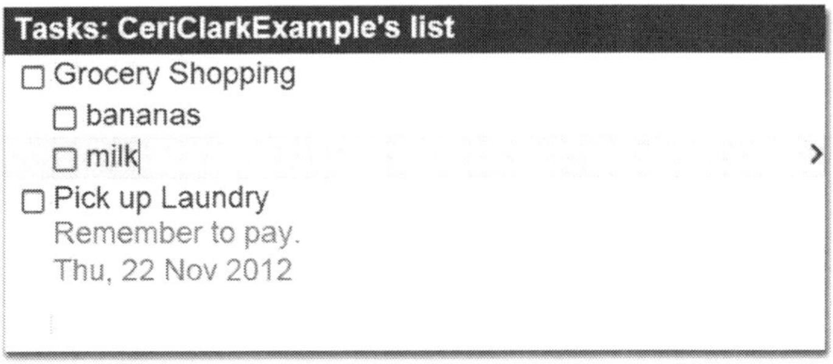

Figure 12.6 Task indenting in action

Move up or down

Similar to indenting, click on the subject > **Actions** > **Move up**/**Move down.**

Edit Details

This option will bring up the details page again. Clicking on the arrow next to each task will do the same thing.

Help

Clicking on this will send you to Google's help pages on using Tasks.

Show tips

This will show you tips in the Tasks window.

Email task list

Have a list which you want your partner or friend to see? Email them the list.

Print task list

This sends your list to your printer.

View completed tasks

This is useful if you just want to see what you have completed organized by date.

Sort by due date

If you have put dates to your tasks, see what you need to complete first.

Clear completed tasks

Just have your uncompleted tasks in your list.

Organising lists

On the bottom bar of the task window click on ☰ to bring up some options for creating and editing task lists. Please see the next figure for the list of options.

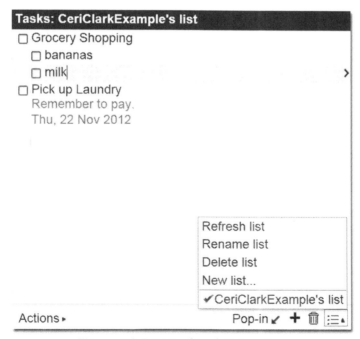

Figure 12.7 List of task list options

Ceri Clark

You can have more than one list, click on the option to choose it from the list that appears when you click on the three lines icon.

Chapter 13 Netiquette

If this is your first email account you may not be familiar with some of the traditions of Netiquette. Here are the top ten rules of email etiquette.

1. Never type your emails ALL IN CAPS LOCK! IT WILL SEEM TO THE READER THAT YOU ARE SHOUTING AT THEM.

2. Don't remove previous messages from your email thread when replying. The person you are emailing may have deleted your previous emails altogether and if you give a short reply without any context they may have no idea what you are talking about.

3. Use a meaningful subject. Should I bother to read this email? If it just says "Howdy", the recipient might think its spam. And at the same time don't send emails with a blank subject either!

4. Don't forward chain-emails, unless it's a *really* funny one.

5. Read the email before you send it. What sounds perfectly reasonable when you are writing can seem really insulting after ten minutes – and that's when you are not trying to be insulting!

117

6. Be careful when replying to mailing lists. Remember that email can go to hundreds if not thousands of people.

7. Don't make personal remarks about people in jest. The reader can't see the glint in your eye as you are being ironic.

8. Don't post your email address on websites unless you want to be sent a lot of spam.

9. Be respectful, imagine you are talking to someone you know. Sending an email can seem anonymous, but people's feelings can still hurt.

10. If you don't know the person you are contacting, try to make your emails as clear and concise as possible. Keep your fonts and language simple. Make sure you do not use yellow, grey or light colors when emailing people. They are difficult to see, why make life hard for people? You may think it looks cool, but if your contact has to highlight, copy it, then paste it into word, change the color and make it bigger just to read it, let's just say your email just may go unread.

Chapter 14 Gmail on your Android Device

With the new Smartphones/Tablets available there is no excuse to ever be without your email. Gmail is so simple to set up with the Android handset. At the time of writing this book I have a Samsung Galaxy S2 so these instructions are designed with that phone in mind. The instructions should be similar across all Android phones and tablets.

Setting up Gmail using the Official Gmail App

Browse your Apps list and find the icon for Gmail. Tapping Menu once you are in it will bring up a list of options.

- Choose **Accounts**, then

- **Add Account** at the bottom of the screen.

- Tap on **Google**

- Read the blurb, then tap on **Next**

- You can **create a Google account** or **Sign in** to an existing one. As we have created one, tap on **Sign in**

- Tap on the username box and type in your full Gmail address

119

- Tap on the password box and type in your password

- Remove the keyboard (Pressing back on your Android device and click on **Sign in**

- Wait

- Choose to **Sync contacts** and/or **Sync Gmail**. Tap on the boxes to the right of the options.

- Wait while it syncs

- Tap on **Finish setup**

Checking Mail in Android

If your phone hasn't sync'd, click on **Menu** and then **Refresh.**

Composing Mail in Android

- Tap on **Menu**

- Choose **Compose**

- Tap on **To**

- Type in the first few letters, if you have sent an email to that person from your phone it will autocomplete the address.

- Add a subject

- Type your message

- Tap on the message icon at the top of the screen

Replying to mail on Android

- Enter an email

- Click on the arrow pointing left on the top right of the screen and fill in the boxes as necessary.

- Clicking on the arrow pointing right will give you the option to forward the message.

Browsing your email using Labels

- Tap on **Menu**

- Tap on **Go to Labels**, then

- Tap the Label you want

Search your email

- Open the **Menu**

- Click on **Search**

- Type in your search term and tap on the magnifying glass.

Other settings

Priority Inbox

By choosing this option you are making the Priority inbox your default inbox. I would recommend you do this only after a couple of months of using your email and you are sure that Google is tagging the right emails as important.

Signature

The Signature you created on the web version of Gmail does not apply on your smartphone. You must create another one here.

Confirm Actions

When you tap to archive, delete or send an email, you can have the app ask you if you are sure. This might save you deleting something you didn't want to delete by accident!

Reply All

You can choose to reply to all in all your messages. This is not recommended.

Auto-advance

Once you have deleted an email, you choose this option to send you to where you want to go next. Do you want to see the next or a previous email or do you want to see all the emails in one list?

Message Text Size

The message text sizes come in Tiny to Huge. Bear in mind that Huge isn't that Huge. They could really do with a Hug*er*!

Batch Operations

Allows more than one action to be done at the same time.

Clear search history

Clearing your search history can save some space on your phone.

Labels

This option allows you to choose how often you want to sync your labels. The options are **sync none**, **sync 4 days** and **sync all.**

Email Notifications

This will put a notification in the status bar to let you know you have new mail.

Select Ringtone

You can choose what ringtone to associate with the email.

Vibrate

Do you want the phone to vibrate when you get a new email message?

Notify Once

This is important if you tend to get a lot of emails at the same time. Rather than get twenty notifications, choosing this will just let you know you have new email not send you twenty notifications one after the other. You just open the Gmail app to see what they are.

Setting up Gmail using MailDroid

There are a couple of 3rd party email apps on Android, the two most popular are K9 and MailDroid after the official Gmail app. I have used all three and after a lot of trial and error I found MailDroid to be the best app by far. If you have a relative or you yourself find the text too small in the main Gmail app, I would suggest you give MailDroid a go.

Installing MailDroid

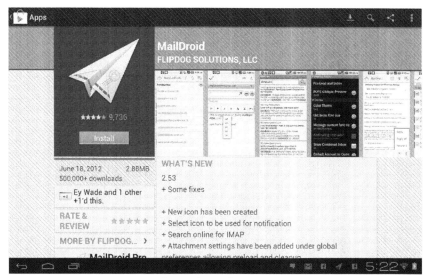

Figure 14.1 MailDroid on the Google Marketplace

There is a free and paid version of MailDroid on the Marketplace. I have the pro version but that is only because I thought the app was so good that I thought the developer should be recompensed for his/her effort. I could have just as easily have used the free version – it has all the options you need.

Click on **Install** and Google Play will let you know what permissions the application requires.

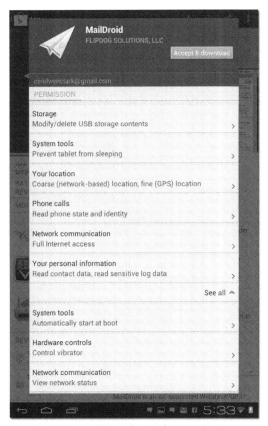

Figure 14.2 MailDroid permissions

Account Setup

Setting up your Google account is simple with MailDroid. Choose **Manual Setup** then **IMAP**.

Figure 14.3 Choose Manual Setup

Type in the information from the figure below (replacing your email address and password with your own) into the fields, then click **Next**. These details are also in the IMAP settings earlier in this book.

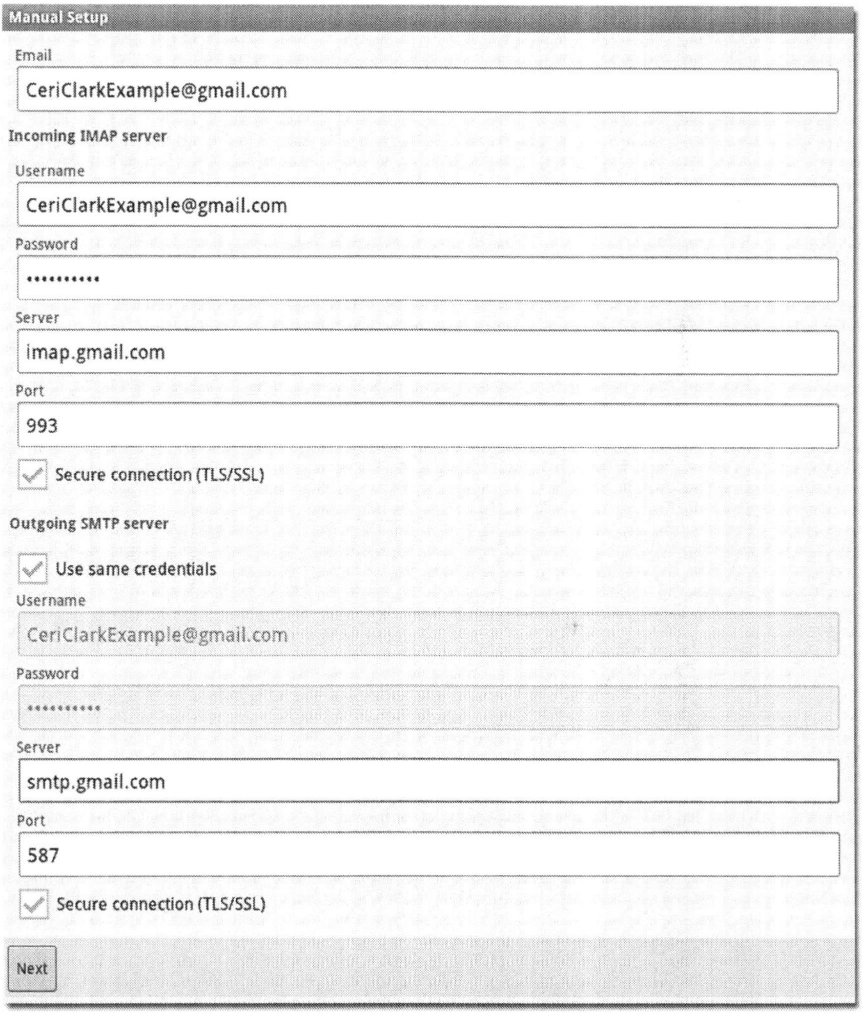

Manual Setup

Email
> CeriClarkExample@gmail.com

Incoming IMAP server

Username
> CeriClarkExample@gmail.com

Password
> ••••••••••

Server
> imap.gmail.com

Port
> 993

☑ Secure connection (TLS/SSL)

Outgoing SMTP server

☑ Use same credentials

Username
> CeriClarkExample@gmail.com

Password
> ••••••••••

Server
> smtp.gmail.com

Port
> 587

☑ Secure connection (TLS/SSL)

Next

Figure 14.4 IMAP settings

Click on your email address under Accounts and you will see the latest email in your Gmail account.

Ceri Clark

Once you have set up your account it is time to go into the settings. MailDroid is extremely customizable and has far too many options to get into here so I will talk about the most useful settings.

Click on Menu > Preferences and the following screen will load:

Figure 14.5 Preferences (Global Settings)

Incidentally, to get to the menu on a device without a physical menu button. Click on the three vertical dots and choose Preferences from there.

Figure 14.6 Menu Icons in MailDroid

The first icon above will start a new email, the second will refresh the email list, the third will allow you to search your email, the fourth will let you add another email account and the three vertical dots icon is the menu button.

Back to **Preferences**, I would keep the conversation mode off, only because I use my mobile device for looking at the latest messages. I login to the website to reply to complicated messages or see the background information. It is easier to see the latest email when the messages are individual.

The other item I would like to draw your attention to from these settings are the font sizes, you can make sure they are bigger here. You can also use pinch-to-zoom within the actual emails but to make the text bigger in lists you need to change the font settings here.

There are another set of settings which are really useful. Click into your email address in MailDroid. Press the **Menu** button and chose **More**, then **Account Preferences**. The next set of settings will appear:

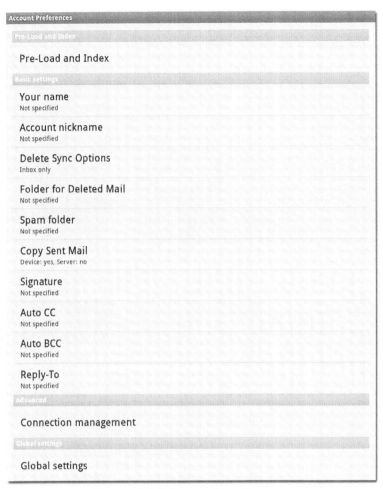

Figure 14.7 Account preferences

The important items to note here are **Your name**, which lets the person you are emailing know who you are and **Account nickname**. This means you can tell apart email accounts if you have more than one picked up by MailDroid. You don't need to mess with the other settings but it can improve your experience if you set them to your preference.

Note, if you choose **Global Settings** that will take you to the previous settings as described earlier in this chapter.

Composing a Message using MailDroid

Click on your email address once you have opened MailDroid. Press your Menu button and choose the first icon which will appear at the top of your screen from the following options:

Figure 14.8 Menu icons

Fill in the fields then click send (the top left icon on the right of the page that looks like a paper airplane). The other icons to note are the abc (spell check), the trash can (to delete/discard your email) and the three vertical dots which denote the menu button.

Figure 14.9 Composing mail in MailDroid

To attach a file, in the open email click on the Menu button and choose **attach file**. Browse your device and select it. Send your email as normal.

Viewing Mail in MailDroid

To view your mail simply select the email you want to look at from the list. If the text is too small, you can use the pinch-to-zoom function on your device by pressing two fingers on the screen and pushing them apart while sliding them on the screen.

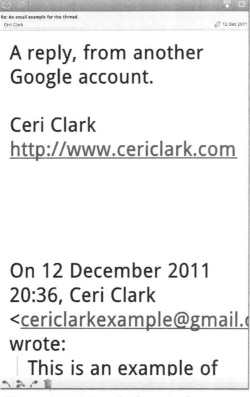

Figure 14.10 Email after pinch-to-zoom

Chapter 15 Advanced Features - Google Labs

Google Labs are experimental features that Google are testing. They may disappear at any time or appear as standard features later on if they become popular. I'm going to go through a select few labs which you may find useful. To find the labs, Click on the gear wheel at the top right of Gmail and then go to Settings > Labs.

Apps Search

Apps Search
by the Apps Search team

Extends search with Google Docs and Sites results. Apps Search will find the most relevant Docs and Sites and show them below Gmail search results.

◉ **Enable**
○ **Disable**

Send feedback

Figure 15.1 Labs Settings - Apps Search

If you use your email as way of saving information as well as Google Docs and find yourself searching two different places, why not combine your search into one easy search? Enabling this lab will mean that you search your docs and it will appear along with your email.

Authentication icon for verified senders

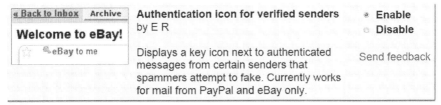

Figure 15.2 Labs Settings - Authentication icons for eBay and PayPal emails

If you are worried about phishing emails for your eBay and PayPal accounts then you HAVE to enable this lab. A small icon will appear next to genuine emails from eBay and PayPal so you don't have to worry that someone is trying to make you click on a link to a fake site.

Create a document

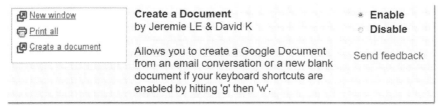

Figure 15.3 Labs Settings - Create a document

This is an extremely useful tool. If you enable this, go to **More** in the toolbar above an open email and choose **Create a document**, then a Google doc will be created with the information from the opened email. If you have a habit of deleting emails by accident this could be a way of preserving important information. It will also be useful if you want to share the information with a friend but you know you will have to add details periodically.

Default 'Reply to all'

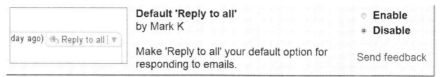

Figure 15.4 Labs Settings - Default 'Reply to all'

Warning, I would not recommend this option. It can seem very convenient to have a reply to all automatically done for you for every email. It means that no one would miss out on your emails if you are replying back but if you are using your Gmail account for business purposes take the lessons learnt from big business that this may not be the best idea. The news has been full in the past of emails sent to the wrong people by accident and then forwarded on to strangers. The type of email that you shouldn't reply to all will usually find their way half-way across the world before you can say jiminy cricket! It is best to think before replying and think twice before replying to all.

Default Text Styling

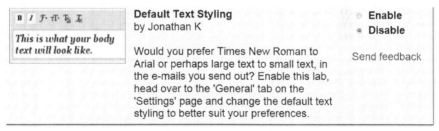

Figure 15.5 Labs Settings - Default Text Styling

Enable this lab by clicking on the circle next to **Enable** then Select **Save Changes** at the bottom of the page. If you always want to send emails with the Arial font or larger text size then if you enable this, it will save you changing the style time after time.

Filter import/export

Figure 15.6 Labs Settings - Filter import/export

If you are or become an advanced user of Filters it is a good idea to backup your settings, you might also want to help a friend out and share your filters with them. Enable this feature to do this.

Flickr previews in mail

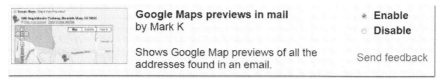

Figure 15.7 Labs Settings - Flickr previews in mail

If you or your friends use Flickr for your photos, this lab will allow you to see a preview of the photo in the email itself. Click on **Enable** then **Save Changes** at the bottom of the email.

Google Maps preview in mail

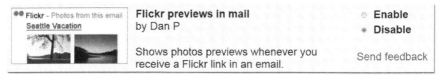

Figure 15.8 Labs Settings - Google Maps preview in mail

If this is enabled, when someone send you an address in an email, a Google Map will automatically load showing where the address is.

Google Voice player in mail

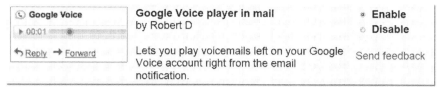

Figure 15.9 Labs Settings - Google voice player in mail

Don't you wish you could play your voicemails from your computer? With this lab you can. Enable this and when someone leaves you a voicemail in your Google Voice account, you can play it from the email.

Inserting images into your email

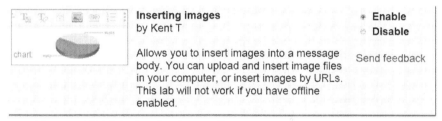

Figure 15.10 Labs Settings - Inserting images in your emails

Probably the most important and useful of the labs. Enabling this will insert a small picture in the formatting bar which will allow you to add pictures inside your emails rather than just attaching them. Click on **Enable** then **Save Changes** at the bottom of the email.

Message Translation

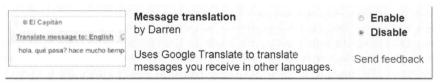

Figure 15.11 Labs Settings - Message translation

Receiving a message in a language you don't understand can be quite frustrating. Rather than copying a message and pasting it into Google Translate, this lab will let you do it straight from the email.

Picasa previews in mail

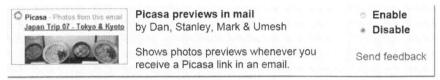

Figure 15.12 Labs Settings - Picasa previews in mail

As in the Flickr lab, this will allow you to see images from Picasa when someone sends you a Picasa link in an email. Click on **Enable** then **Save Changes** at the bottom of the email.

Pictures in chat

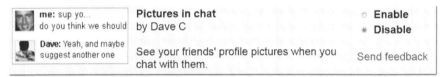

Figure 15.13 Labs Settings - Pictures in chat

Chat can be pretty boring with just text. Enable this lab to see your friend's pictures while chatting to them. Click on **Enable** then **Save Changes** at the bottom of the email.

Preview Pane

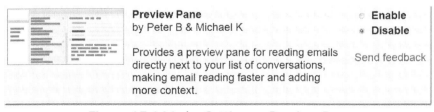

Figure 15.14 Labs Settings - Preview Pane

Do you miss the preview pane in Outlook and other traditional email programs? This lab allows you to get the familiar style inside Gmail. When you check a box in your list view you will be able to see the contents of the email in the Preview Pane.

Once you have enabled the Preview you need to use the dropdown button on the top right of the screen and choose vertical or horizontal view as seen at the top of the next figure.

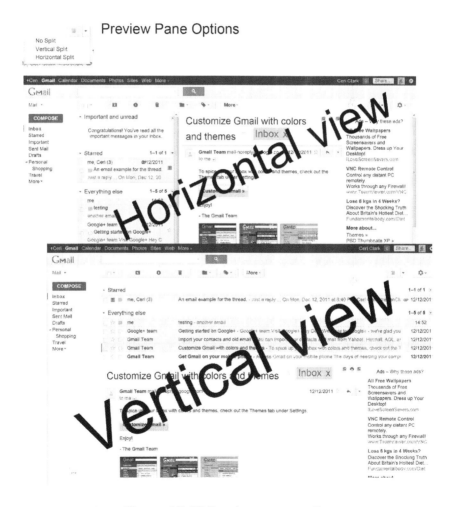

Figure 15.15 Preview pane options

Send & Archive

Figure 15.16 Labs Settings - Send & Archive

When you reply to a message and send, the discussion/message stays in the inbox until you archive the message. This lab put a button when you are composing your mail so that you can save and archive at the same time, tidying your inbox.

Sender Time Zone

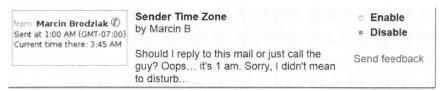

Figure 15.17 Labs Settings - Sender Time Zone

This is useful if you have contacts abroad who live in a different time zone. It lets you know what the time is where they are. There may be a reason why they haven't replied within an hour if it is 2am there!

Undo Send

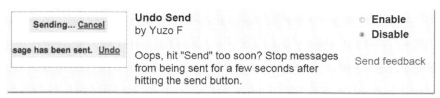

Figure 15.18 Labs Settings - Undo Send

This is a lab I could have done with a few times in my life but it only works for a couple of seconds. Stop that email from leaving your account. Click on **Enable** then **Save Changes** at the bottom of the email. All these labs can be enabled or disabled at any time.

Ceri Clark

Chapter 16 Frequently Asked Questions (FAQ)

What was the address again to login to Gmail?

http://mail.google.com or http://gmail.com

Help I've lost my password, what do I do now?

You've been on holiday or have had better things to do than check your email. You've opened up Gmail and you can't remember your password. This screen shows up:

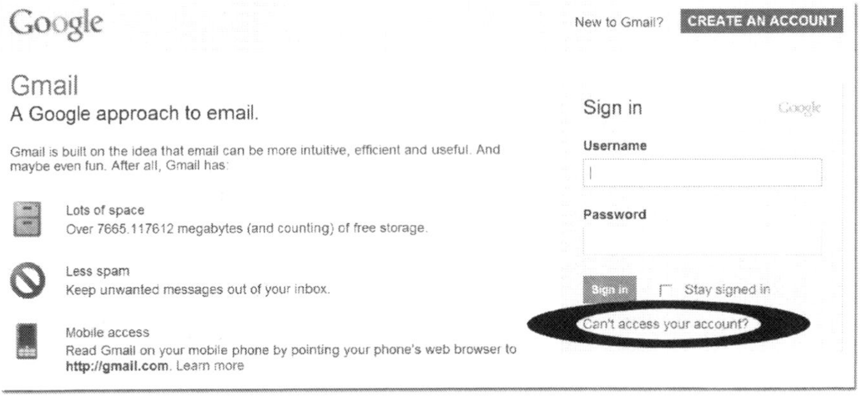

Google

New to Gmail? **CREATE AN ACCOUNT**

Gmail
A Google approach to email.

Gmail is built on the idea that email can be more intuitive, efficient and useful. And maybe even fun. After all, Gmail has:

Lots of space
Over 7665.117612 megabytes (and counting) of free storage.

Less spam
Keep unwanted messages out of your inbox.

Mobile access
Read Gmail on your mobile phone by pointing your phone's web browser to **http://gmail.com**. Learn more

Sign in   Google

Username

Password

Sign in   ☐ Stay signed in

Can't access your account?

Figure 16.1 Where to go if you have lost your password

Fear not, click on **Can't access your email?** (Circled above).

The following screen will load:

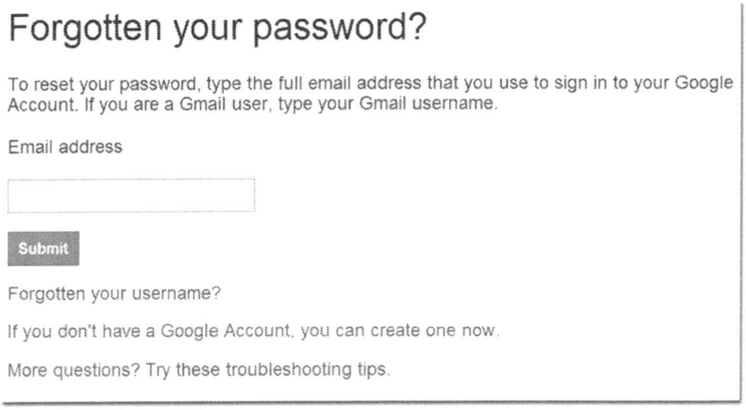

Forgotten your password?

To reset your password, type the full email address that you use to sign in to your Google Account. If you are a Gmail user, type your Gmail username.

Email address

Submit

Forgotten your username?

If you don't have a Google Account, you can create one now.

More questions? Try these troubleshooting tips.

Figure 16.2 Forgotten your password screen

Type in your email address and then press **Submit**. You will be asked to type in some characters to make sure you are a person and not some internet robot, hell bent on your email destruction. Once this has been done, your password will be sent to an alternative email account. If you don't have an alternate email address (and I suggest you have one other if only for mailing lists and the like) then you can click next to **I no longer have access to this**. Then click on continue. As this is the password recovery of last resort, Google will ask you lots of information to verify your identity. Take my advice and have a 'spam' account with another email provider!

Where do I go to change my password?

Go to Settings > Account and Import > Change password.

Do I need a special browser to use Gmail?

Gmail runs on most browsers including Internet Explorer, Firefox, Chrome and Safari.

How do I print email?

This is easy. Enter the email you want to print. Look for the grey box on the top right of the email. Click on the arrow next to reply and select Print.

If there are any questions you would like answered about Gmail that you think should be in this guide, visit http://www.CeriClark.com and have a look at my contact page. I will update this ebook with the new addition to the FAQ.

Ceri Clark

Index

ABOUT THE AUTHOR

Ceri Clark has worked in information and libraries for over 11 years. In her career she produced several in-house guides to help clients use technology and internet services as part of her day job before publishing guides with Lycan Books.

As well as *A Simpler Guide to the best free Android Apps* and *A Simpler Guide to Gmail* she has also written her debut fiction novel, *Children of the Elementi*.

Made in the USA
Lexington, KY
28 November 2012